Dementia

A Personal Roadmap to Hope and Healing

Explore Groundbreaking Advances in Research, Early Detection, and Innovative Treatments That Offer a Promising Future

Debra Lewis RN,BSN

© **Copyright Debra Lewis RN, BSN 2025 - All rights reserved.**

The content within this book may not be reproduced, duplicated or transmitted without direct written permission from the author or the publisher.

Under no circumstances will any blame or legal responsibility be held against the publisher, or author, for any damages, reparation, or monetary loss due to the information contained within this book. Either directly or indirectly. You are responsible for your own choices, actions, and results.

Legal Notice:

This book is copyright protected. This book is only for personal use. You cannot amend, distribute, sell, use, quote or paraphrase any part, of the content within this book, without the consent of the author or publisher.

Disclaimer Notice:

Please note the information contained within this document is for educational and entertainment purposes only. All effort has been expended to present accurate, up-to-date, and reliable, complete information. No warranties of any kind are declared or implied. Readers acknowledge that the author is not engaging in the rendering of legal, financial, medical or professional advice. The content within this book has been derived from various sources. Please consult a licensed professional before attempting any techniques outlined in this book.

By reading this document, the reader agrees that under no circumstances is the author responsible for any losses, direct or indirect, which are incurred as a result of the use of the information contained within this document, including, but not limited to, — errors, omissions, or inaccuracies.

Contents

Foreword	5
Introduction	7
1. THE FOUNDATIONS OF DEMENTIA	15
Differentiating Dementia Types	16
Risk Factors for Dementia	20
2. UNDERSTANDING THE DIFFERENCE	29
Dementia and Cognitive Decline	
Normal Aging	30
Self-Assessment	37
3. EARLY DETECTION AND DIAGNOSIS	41
Biomarkers	41
Brain Imaging	43
Blood Tests	46
Cerebrospinal Fluid (CSF) Tests	47
Genetic Risk Profiling	48
AI in Diagnosis	49
4. LIFESTYLE INTERVENTIONS FOR PREVENTION	53
Neuroplasticity and Cognitive Reserve	53
Physical Activity	56
Mental Stimulation	58
Nutrition	59
5. TREATMENT ADVANCES AND EMERGING THERAPIES	65
FDA-Approved Medications to Treat Alzheimer's	66
FDA-Approved Medications to Manage Symptoms	71
Emerging Treatments	74
6. HOLISTIC APPROACHES TO DEMENTIA CARE	77
Cognitive Stimulation Therapy (CST)	77
Transcranial Magnetic Stimulation (TMS)	81

Acupuncture and Acupressure	82
Mindfulness-Based Interventions	84

7. TECHNOLOGICAL INNOVATIONS IN DEMENTIA CARE	91
Pathways to Improve Caregiving	92
Adapting Technology Use According to Disease Stage	96
Limitations of Technology	98

8. ETHICAL CONSIDERATIONS IN DEMENTIA CARE	101
Complexities in Communicating the Diagnosis	102
Genetic and Biomarker Testing in Dementia Ethics	104
Decision-Making and Capacity Assessment Ethics	107
Symptom and Behavioral Management Ethics	110
Cultural and Societal Ethics	114
The Ethics of Artificial Intelligence	118

9. EMPOWERING THOSE AFFECTED BY DEMENTIA	123
Defining Empowerment in the Context of Dementia	124
Implications for Practice	129

10. EMOTIONAL SUPPORT FOR THOSE AFFECTED BY DEMENTIA	131
Support for the Person with a Dementia Diagnosis	132
Support for the Family	133
Support for the Caregiver	138

Conclusion	143
References	147
About the Author	151

Foreword

Dementia is more than just a medical condition—it is a journey that profoundly affects not only those diagnosed but also the families, friends, and caregivers who walk beside them. Debra Lewis takes on a journey of education through her world as seen while caring for her parents, who both passed due to dementia.

In today's world, memory-related illnesses are becoming increasingly prevalent, challenging us to rethink the way we support and care for our aging loved ones.

Advances in science offer hope, but true comfort comes from the human connection—compassion, patience, and unwavering love. As we navigate this evolving landscape, we must remember that even when memories fade, the essence of a person remains.

Through education, understanding, and heartfelt caregiving, we can provide dignity, joy, and meaning in every stage of life. This book is a beacon of light for those on this path, offering guidance, wisdom, and the reassurance that no one is alone in this journey.

As the Director/Partner of Visiting Angels of Northern Arizona I have witnessed the past 5 years a Senior Tsunami coming especially in the USA.

Time to be proactive and read Debra's books.

Cecelia Jernegan
Director/Partner Visiting Angels of Northern Arizona

Introduction

In 2020, over 55 million people worldwide were living with dementia, with a new diagnosis every three seconds. As a result, the number of people suffering with dementia is projected to double every 20 years, reaching 78 million by 2030 and 139 million by 2050 (Alzheimer's Disease International, n.d.).

It's easy to see these statistics as just numbers. But they are more than that. They represent people struggling, lives disrupted, families heartbroken, and a global challenge that demands our attention. Dementia is a neurological condition that develops when brain cells, known as neurons, become damaged. These neurons play a vital role in essential human functions, including thinking, walking, speaking, and, most notably, memory.

Already, dementia is the seventh leading cause of death in the world and one of the largest causes of disability and dependency among older people (Alzheimer's Association, 2024). As our population ages, understanding and addressing dementia becomes more urgent than ever.

This book aims to provide you with the latest advances in dementia research, detection, and treatment. I focus on what's new and cutting-edge. I am avoiding caregiver or legal topics as I have already addressed these in my first book, *Dementia Caregiving 101*. I want to keep our attention sharply on the science and medicine of dementia. Whether you're concerned about your or a loved one's cognitive health or eager to understand more about this condition, this book is designed to offer practical and insightful information.

At the heart of my exploration is a simple thesis: Advancements in research are transforming how we understand and manage dementia. Genetic insights, lifestyle interventions, and technological breakthroughs are paving the way for better prevention and treatment strategies. By unpacking these developments, I aim to reshape our approach to cognitive health, making it more proactive and informed.

In "Chapter 1: The Foundations of Dementia," readers will be introduced to dementia, beginning with a discussion of the different types of dementia and the key differences between them. The chapter explains the risk factors for dementia, dividing them into non-modifiable and modifiable categories. Non-modifiable factors, such as age and genetics, are explored to help readers understand the aspects of dementia that cannot be controlled, while modifiable factors, such as lifestyle choices, are discussed to provide insight into how certain behaviors or environmental factors may influence the development of dementia. This chapter provides essential background information, offering a solid foundation for understanding the disease and its causes.

In "Chapter 2: Understanding the Difference – Dementia and Cognitive Decline," the book differentiates between normal age-related cognitive decline and dementia. It highlights the changes that occur in the brain and body as part of normal aging, such as cognitive slowing and sensory changes, which are often confused with early symptoms of dementia. The chapter will also help readers assess their own cognitive health, offering practical advice for recognizing the early signs of dementia, such as memory impairment, difficulty with communication, and noticeable behavioral changes. This understanding is key to distinguishing between natural aging and the onset of dementia.

"Chapter 3: Early Detection and Diagnosis" looks at the importance of early diagnosis and the tools available for detecting dementia. Readers will learn about biomarkers, various brain imaging techniques (including structural, functional, and molecular imaging), and the role of blood tests and cerebrospinal fluid tests in diagnosing dementia. The chapter also discusses genetic risk profiling and the innovative use of artificial intelligence (AI) in diagnosis.

In "Chapter 4: Lifestyle Interventions for Prevention," the focus shifts to lifestyle choices that can help prevent or delay the onset of dementia. The concept of neuroplasticity and cognitive reserve is explained, highlighting how the brain's ability to adapt and compensate for damage can be strengthened through healthy behaviors. The chapter discusses the benefits of physical activity, mental stimulation, and proper nutrition, with a special emphasis on diets such as the Mediterranean and MIND diets. These interventions promote overall brain health and help reduce the risk of cognitive decline.

"Chapter 5: Treatment Advances and Emerging Therapies" explores the most current advancements in the treatment of dementia. This chapter provides a detailed overview of FDA-approved medications for treating Alzheimer's disease, including drugs like lecanemab and donanemab. It also covers medications used to manage symptoms, such as donepezil, memantine, and rivastigmine. Emerging treatments, such as therapeutic plasma exchange, efforts to prevent tau tangling, and reducing inflammation, will be discussed. The chapter also investigates the growing understanding of the gut-brain connection, insulin resistance, and the heart-brain link, as well as the potential role of hormones in dementia treatment.

In "Chapter 6: Holistic Approaches to Dementia Care," readers will learn about various non-pharmacological therapies that are gaining recognition in dementia care. Cognitive stimulation therapy, music therapy, art therapy, and reminiscence therapy will be explored, showing how these approaches can enhance cognitive function and improve the quality of life for individuals with dementia. Additionally, the chapter examines transcranial magnetic stimulation, acupuncture, acupressure, and mindfulness-based interventions, all of which have shown promise in managing symptoms and improving the well-being of patients.

"Chapter 7: Technological Innovations in Dementia Care" discusses the role of technology in improving dementia care. The chapter focuses on how advancements such as cognitive offloading, automated task management, and remote monitoring can support caregivers and patients. It explores how emotional and social support can be enhanced through technology and outlines the potential benefits of adapting technology use at different stages of dementia. Limitations of technology will also be addressed to give readers a balanced perspective on its capabilities and challenges.

In "Chapter 8: Ethical Considerations in Dementia Care," the book tackles the complex ethical issues surrounding dementia care. Topics include the challenges of communicating a dementia diagnosis, the ethics of truth-telling, and the use of genetic and biomarker testing. The chapter also explores decision-making and capacity assessment, the process of advance care planning, and managing symptoms and behaviors in the different stages of dementia. Ethical dilemmas, such as physician-hastened death requests and financial, caregiver, and societal impacts of dementia, will also be discussed, alongside the role of artificial intelligence in dementia care and the need for ethical guidelines in these practices.

"Chapter 9: Empowering Those Affected by Dementia" emphasizes the importance of empowerment for individuals with dementia. The chapter defines what it means to be empowered in the context of dementia and discusses how empowerment can positively influence both individuals with dementia and their caregivers. It also explores the role of the environment in supporting empowerment and outlines the effects of empowerment on various aspects of the dementia experience. This chapter provides valuable insight into fostering a sense of control and dignity for those affected by dementia.

Finally, in "Chapter 10: Emotional Support for Those Affected by Dementia," readers will gain an understanding of the emotional challenges faced by individuals with dementia and their families. The chapter discusses strategies for providing emotional support to both patients and their families, with a special focus on understanding the reactions of children to a family member's diagnosis. It also addresses the often-overlooked issue of caregiver burnout, offering practical solutions for managing stress and preventing burnout. The chapter provides essential guidance for caregivers to ensure their well-being while caring for their loved ones.

My goal is to empower you with knowledge. Whether you're worried about your cognitive health or seeking ways to support someone affected by dementia, this book provides insights into the latest research and practical approaches. I will give you the tools to make informed decisions and understand the complex factors at play in cognitive health.

Let me introduce myself. I am a registered nurse with 35 years of experience. I am also a daughter and caregiver to both my parents before they passed from dementia. I'm a passionate advocate for helping adults navigate the challenges of dementia. With years of experience in this field, I strive to deliver clear, reputable guidance that anyone can follow. My focus is on the latest breakthroughs, from genetic research to advanced imaging techniques, to help you make informed choices about prevention and care. The topics discussed here are by no means all-encompassing. I have just scratched the surface of what is happening around the world.

As you read, expect to gain actionable insights into managing and understanding dementia. You'll deepen your understanding of complex topics and learn how to apply this knowledge in your life. This book is about empowering you to take control of your cognitive health and make decisions that align with the latest scientific findings.

I invite you to engage actively with the content. Reflect on the insights provided and consider how you can apply this knowledge in your life or support others affected by dementia. The journey through this book is not just about reading; it's about understanding, applying, and sharing what you learn. Let's navigate the complexities of dementia together, with curiosity and a commitment to understanding.

Chapter 1

The Foundations of Dementia

Did you know that dementia isn't a single disease but rather a term that covers a range of specific medical conditions? Each of these conditions has its own unique characteristics, symptoms, and progression patterns. Understanding these differences is the first step for anyone looking to grasp the complexities of dementia. This chapter aims to break down these distinctions so you can better comprehend how each type impacts individuals differently. We often hear about dementia in broad terms, but delving into the specifics helps demystify this challenging topic. We will also cover the risk factors that increase the likelihood of an individual developing dementia. This will include non-modifiable risk factors, such as age and genetics, as well as modifiable factors, such as education, diet, and lifestyle.

Differentiating Dementia Types

Alzheimer's disease is the leading cause of dementia, responsible for 60% to 80% of cases. The disease develops as beta-amyloid plaques accumulate outside neurons and twisted tau protein strands form inside them. This process will be explained in greater detail later in this chapter. These abnormalities lead to widespread neuronal death, brain atrophy, and inflammation, progressively impairing cognitive and motor functions. The earliest symptoms typically involve difficulty recalling recent conversations, names, and events. Over time, individuals may develop apathy, depression, confusion, and impaired judgment. As the disease advances, motor function deteriorates, causing difficulty with walking, speaking, and swallowing. These symptoms significantly interfere with independent living, requiring increasing levels of care and assistance (Alzheimer's Association, 2024).

Vascular dementia, otherwise known as cerebrovascular disease, contributes to 5% to 10% of dementia cases and occurs due to damage to blood vessels in the brain. When the brain does not receive enough blood, oxygen, and nutrients, neurons die, leading to cognitive decline. This condition often manifests as slowed thinking, impaired decision-making, and difficulty with planning or organizing. Unlike Alzheimer's, which initially affects memory, vascular dementia primarily disrupts executive functions, which are the higher-order mental processes that coordinate behavior. However, as the disease progresses, memory impairment may develop, and motor difficulties, such as problems with gait and balance, can emerge. Vascular dementia often coexists with Alzheimer's disease, a condition referred to as mixed dementia. The presence of both diseases exacerbates cognitive decline, making diagnosis and treatment more complex (Alzheimer's Association, 2024).

Hippocampal sclerosis (HS) affects 3% to 13% of dementia patients and results from the shrinkage and hardening of tissue in the hippocampus, a brain region responsible for memory formation. Individuals with HS experience significant memory loss, which can lead to a misdiagnosis of Alzheimer's disease. However, HS differs from Alzheimer's in its pathology and progression. While Alzheimer's disease involves widespread brain atrophy and cognitive impairment beyond memory, HS primarily affects episodic memory—the memory of our experiences—while sparing other cognitive functions in the early stages. The condition is most common in individuals over 85, suggesting that age-related factors may contribute to its development. In some cases, HS occurs alongside other dementias, further complicating diagnosis and treatment (Alzheimer's Association, 2024).

Lewy body dementia (LBD) accounts for approximately 5% of dementia cases and is associated with abnormal deposits of alpha-synuclein protein, known as Lewy bodies, inside nerve cells. These deposits disrupt cognitive functions, behavior, mood, and motor control. Individuals with LBD often experience early symptoms such as sleep disturbances, vivid visual hallucinations, and visuospatial impairment. As the disease progresses, Parkinson-like symptoms, such as tremors, muscle stiffness, and slow movement, may develop. Unlike other dementias, LBD symptoms can fluctuate dramatically, with individuals having periods of relative clarity followed by episodes of severe confusion. This unpredictability poses challenges for both individuals with LBD and their caregivers, requiring flexibility and resilience in providing care (Alzheimer's Association, 2024).

Frontotemporal dementia (FTD) accounts for approximately 3% of dementia cases in individuals over 65 and 10% in those under 65. This form of dementia results from nerve cell death in the frontal and temporal lobes, causing these brain regions to shrink. The condition leads to profound personality, behavioral, and language changes, distinguishing it from Alzheimer's disease, which primarily affects memory in its early stages. Individuals with FTD may exhibit impulsive or socially inappropriate behavior, apathy, or emotional detachment. Language difficulties, including difficulty understanding or producing speech, are also common. Since memory typically remains intact in the early stages, FTD can be misdiagnosed as a psychiatric disorder rather than a neurodegenerative disease. This form of dementia primarily affects individuals between the ages of 45 and 60, disrupting careers, relationships, and family life at a stage when many are still actively engaged in work and personal responsibilities (Alzheimer's Association, 2024).

Distinguishing between these types of dementia can be challenging due to symptom overlap. For example, the memory issues seen in Alzheimer's might also appear in vascular dementia, while the movement issues in Lewy body dementia can mimic those in Parkinson's disease. This overlap complicates diagnosis, making it important for healthcare providers to conduct thorough assessments.

Here is a comparison table outlining the key differences between the major types of dementia:

	Alzheimer's Disease	Vascular Dementia	Hippocampal Sclerosis (HS)	Lewy Body Dementia (LBD)	Fronto-temporal Dementia (FTD)
Cause	Accumulation of beta-amyloid plaques and twisted tau protein strands, leading to neuronal death and brain atrophy.	Damage to blood vessels in the brain, reducing blood and oxygen supply to brain tissue.	Shrinkage and hardening of tissue in the hippocampus, impairing memory function.	Abnormal deposits of alpha-synuclein protein (Lewy bodies) inside nerve cells.	Nerve cell death in the frontal and temporal lobes, leading to brain shrinkage.
Primary Symptoms	Early: Memory loss (recent events, names), apathy, depression, confusion, poor judgment. Later: Motor difficulties (walking, speaking, swallowing).	Slowed thinking, impaired decision-making, difficulty planning and organizing. Memory loss develops later. Motor problems (gait, balance) may emerge.	Memory loss, especially related to recent events, with minimal impairment of other cognitive functions.	Early: Vivid visual hallucinations, sleep disturbances, visuospatial impairment. Later: Motor symptoms like tremors and rigidity, resembling Parkinson's disease.	Early: Significant personality and behavioral changes, inappropriate social behavior, emotional detachment, apathy, and language difficulties. Memory is initially spared.
Progression	Gradual and progressive decline over years.	Stepwise decline due to multiple strokes or progressive vascular damage.	Slowly progressive, often seen in older adults.	Symptoms fluctuate, with good and bad days. Progression varies.	Progressive but can vary in speed depending on the subtype.
Common Age Group	Most common in individuals over 65.	More common in individuals over 65, especially after strokes or cardiovascular events.	Most common in individuals over 85.	Most common in individuals over 60.	Most common between ages 45-60.

Understanding the distinctions among dementia types empowers you to navigate the complexities of diagnosis and treatment. As we explore these different forms of dementia, remember that knowledge is power. By understanding the nuances of each type, you can become an informed advocate for yourself or your loved ones, ensuring that the care provided aligns with the specific needs dictated by the type of dementia present.

Risk Factors for Dementia

Non-Modifiable Risk Factors

Age

The likelihood of developing Alzheimer's dementia rises sharply with age. Research indicates that 5% of individuals aged 65 to 74, 13.2% of those aged 75 to 84, and 33.4% of those aged 85 or older develop the disease (Alzheimer's Association, 2024).

APOE4 Gene

Alzheimer's disease usually does not stem from a single genetic cause. Instead, multiple genes interact with lifestyle and environmental factors to influence a person's risk. As a result, someone may carry several genetic variants that either increase or reduce the likelihood of developing Alzheimer's.

However, one of the most significant genetic risk factors is a version of the apolipoprotein E (APOE) gene known as APOE4. Genes serve as instructions for the body, and the APOE gene plays a role in moving cholesterol and other fats through the bloodstream (National Institute on Aging, 2021).

The APOE gene exists in three main forms:

- **APOE3:** The most common version, which does not seem to influence Alzheimer's risk.
- **APOE2:** A rarer version, which may actually provide some protection against Alzheimer's.

- **APOE4:** Linked to a higher risk of developing Alzheimer's disease.

Each person inherits two copies of the APOE gene, one from each biological parent. These copies can combine in six possible ways: 2/2, 2/3, 2/4, 3/3, 3/4, and 4/4. Having two copies of APOE4 leads to a greater risk of developing Alzheimer's than having just one copy. However, carrying APOE4 does not guarantee that a person will develop the disease, as some people with this genetic variant never experience symptoms.

Approximately 25% of people carry one copy of APOE4, while 2% to 3% carry two copies (National Institute on Aging, 2021).

The influence of APOE and other genetic variants on Alzheimer's risk also varies across different populations. Research suggests that genetic ancestry affects the degree of risk, so the impact of genetic variants may differ among individuals of African, Asian, American Indian, and European descent (National Institute on Aging, n.d.). Ongoing studies aim to clarify how specific genetic variants contribute to Alzheimer's risk within different groups and to develop treatments and prevention strategies tailored to each population.

Scientists do not yet fully understand why APOE4 increases Alzheimer's risk. One theory suggests that it disrupts lipid metabolism—the process cells use to manage and use fats (National Institute on Aging, 2021). Lipids are crucial for brain function because they help form cell membranes, store energy, and transport molecules. When lipid metabolism is disrupted, it may lead to harmful changes in the brain.

However, inheriting the APOE4 variant does not guarantee that an individual will develop Alzheimer's. In 2022, researchers identified 31 additional genes that influence biological processes associated with Alzheimer's (Alzheimer's Association, 2024).

Lipid Imbalances

Recent studies suggest that lipid imbalances may be a key contributor to Alzheimer's disease. When brain cells fail to properly manage fats, they can accumulate harmful deposits, interfering with essential functions. Scientists believe this disruption may contribute to the formation of amyloid plaques, one of the defining features of Alzheimer's disease. Amyloid plaques are clumps of protein that build up in the brain and disrupt communication between neurons. In people with Alzheimer's, these plaques cause brain cells to function poorly and eventually die, leading to memory loss and cognitive decline (National Institute on Aging, 2021).

Dr. Li-Huei Tsai and the late Dr. Susan Lindquist of MIT led a study investigating how APOE4 affects lipid metabolism in brain cells. The researchers used induced pluripotent stem cells (iPSCs), which are reprogrammed human skin cells that can develop into any cell type. They directed these stem cells to become astrocytes, a type of brain cell that produces the most APOE. When examining these APOE4 astrocytes, the researchers discovered excessive lipid buildup, particularly triglycerides, a type of fat. These triglycerides contained more unsaturated fatty acid chains than normal, suggesting a problem with fat processing. When the researchers transformed the stem cells into microglia (another type of brain cell), they found similar lipid metabolism problems, indicating that the disruption was widespread.

To confirm their findings, the researchers conducted an experiment using yeast cells. Yeast and humans share similar lipid metabolism pathways, making yeast a useful model for studying how genes affect fat processing. When they introduced the human APOE4 gene into yeast cells, they observed the same abnormal lipid accumulation that occurred in the human astrocytes. They then ran genetic screenings to identify which pathways were disrupted and found a molecular pathway linked to phospholipid production that was not functioning properly.

Phospholipids are essential components of cell membranes, and disruptions in their production may contribute to Alzheimer's risk. The researchers tested whether increasing phospholipid production could reverse the lipid buildup in APOE4 cells. They discovered that adding choline, a nutrient that helps produce phospholipids, restored normal lipid metabolism in both yeast and human APOE4 astrocytes. This suggests that choline supplementation may be a potential way to reduce the harmful effects of APOE4 on lipid metabolism.

Dr. Tsai emphasized that future research should examine whether APOE4 carriers who take choline supplements in sufficient amounts experience a lower risk of developing Alzheimer's disease.

Although these findings are promising, researchers caution that results observed in isolated cells do not always translate into effective treatments for humans. Further studies are needed to determine whether choline supplementation could have meaningful benefits for people at risk of Alzheimer's disease.

Genetic Mutations

In rare cases, genetic mutations cause Alzheimer's, accounting for less than 1% of all cases (Alzheimer's Association, 2024). Among the genetic variants linked to Alzheimer's, three rare single-gene mutations directly cause the disease:

- **Amyloid precursor protein (APP)** on chromosome 21
- **Presenilin 1 (PSEN1)** on chromosome 14
- **Presenilin 2 (PSEN2)** on chromosome 1 (National Institute on Aging, n.d.).

A child who inherits one of these mutations from a biological parent has a 50% chance of carrying the altered gene. If they inherit the mutation, they have a high probability of developing Alzheimer's before age 65, sometimes much earlier. Cases of Alzheimer's that appear before age 65 are known as early-onset Alzheimer's or sometimes younger-onset Alzheimer's. Less than 10% of all Alzheimer's cases develop this early, and among those who do, 10% to 15% are linked to mutations in APP, PSEN1, and PSEN2 (National Institute on Aging, n.d.).

Mutations in these three genes lead to the production of abnormal proteins that contribute to the disease. Each mutation affects the processing of APP, a protein whose full function remains unclear. When APP breaks down, it produces sticky amyloid fragments, which clump together to form plaques in the brain (National Institute on Aging, n.d.).

Beyond these three genetic mutations, individuals with Down syndrome face a higher risk of developing early-onset Alzheimer's. Down syndrome results from an extra copy of chromosome 21, which carries the APP gene. As a result, many people with Down syndrome experience Alzheimer's-related symptoms in their 50s or 60s. Estimates suggest that at least 50% of people with Down syndrome will develop Alzheimer's (National Institute on Aging, n.d.).

Family History

Many people who develop Alzheimer's have no family history of the disease. However, those with a parent or sibling who has been diagnosed face a higher risk than those without a direct family connection. One large study found that individuals with a parent who had dementia faced a higher risk even when researchers accounted for known genetic factors like APOE-e4. This may be because family history reflects both genetic predisposition and shared lifestyle factors, such as dietary habits and physical activity (Alzheimer's Association, 2024).

Modifiable Risk Factors

Although age, genetics, and family history remain unchangeable, several factors can lower the risk of cognitive decline and dementia. These factors include physical activity, smoking cessation, education, social and mental engagement, blood pressure management, and a healthy diet. The Lancet Commission on dementia prevention reported that modifiable risk factors may contribute to up to 40% of dementia cases. A 2022 study supported this claim, estimating that 37% of dementia cases in the United States stemmed from eight modifiable factors. Among these, midlife obesity, physical inactivity, and low educational attainment stood out as the most significant (Alzheimer's Association, 2024).

Cardiovascular Health

Heart and blood vessel health directly impact brain function. Stroke, which results from blocked or ruptured blood vessels in the brain, significantly increases dementia risk. Conditions like hypertension, diabetes, and smoking, which contribute to cardiovascular disease, also raise the likelihood of dementia. On the other hand, physical activity supports cardiovascular health and may help protect against dementia. Although researchers have yet to determine the exact types and amounts of physical activity that offer the most protection, evidence suggests that a healthy diet also plays a role. Diets such as the Mediterranean, DASH (Dietary Approaches to Stop Hypertension), and MIND (Mediterranean-DASH Intervention for Neurodegenerative Delay) diets appear to support brain health. However, researchers need further studies to confirm their effectiveness in preventing dementia (Alzheimer's Association, 2024).

Education

Studies consistently show that individuals with higher levels of formal education experience a lower risk of Alzheimer's and other dementias. Education appears to help maintain cognitive function later in life, delaying the onset of symptoms. Researchers explain this trend through the concept of "cognitive reserve," which refers to the brain's ability to adapt to damage while continuing to function. Furthermore, formal education often correlates with socioeconomic status, which influences access to healthcare, physical activity, and nutrition. Those with fewer years of education often belong to lower socioeconomic groups, where higher rates of diabetes, hypertension, and smoking combine with reduced access to health-promoting resources (Alzheimer's Association, 2024).

Social Engagement

Staying socially and mentally engaged may also protect brain health. Participating in stimulating activities can help build cognitive reserve, potentially lowering dementia risk. However, researchers recognize that undiagnosed cognitive impairment may reduce an individual's ability or motivation to engage socially or mentally. This complexity makes it difficult to determine the exact relationship between social engagement and dementia risk. Sensory loss can also play a role. When individuals lose sensory abilities, their mobility and social interaction decrease, further increasing dementia risk (National Institute on Aging, 2023b).

Brain Injury

Head injuries significantly affect dementia risk. Traumatic brain injuries, resulting from falls or blows to the head, increase the likelihood of developing dementia. The severity of the injury influences the level of risk, with moderate to severe injuries leading to a greater chance of cognitive decline. Repetitive brain trauma, which often occurs in contact sports, raises the risk of chronic traumatic encephalopathy (CTE). Although CTE shares some characteristics with Alzheimer's disease, it remains a distinct condition (Alzheimer's Association, 2024).

Sleep Quality

Poor sleep quality also contributes to cognitive decline and Alzheimer's disease. Sleep plays an important role in clearing beta-amyloid and other toxins from the brain. Sleep disorders, such as sleep apnea and insomnia, can interfere with this process and negatively impact memory and attention. As such, research indicates that people who suffer from sleep disorders are at a higher risk of Alzheimer's later in life (Bryant, 2021). Research also suggests that sleep and Alzheimer's disease have a bidirectional relationship. Poor sleep increases dementia risk, while Alzheimer's-related brain changes further disrupt sleep patterns (Alzheimer's Association, 2024).

Air Pollution

Emerging studies indicate that long-term exposure to air pollution, particularly fine particulate matter (PM2.5), may lead to cognitive decline and dementia. PM2.5 particles, produced by combustion processes, can penetrate deep into the lungs and potentially harm brain function. Research has linked prolonged exposure to PM2.5 with faster cognitive decline, reduced brain volume, and higher dementia rates. Although scientists have not yet determined the precise mechanism behind this connection, evidence continues to raise concerns about air pollution's impact on cognitive health (Alzheimer's Association, 2024).

Chapter 2

Understanding the Difference
Dementia and Cognitive Decline

Aging is a natural part of life, bringing with it both physical and cognitive changes. As we grow older, our hair gradually turns gray, our skin develops wrinkles, and our muscle and bone density decrease. Cognitive functions also shift, leading to slower information processing and the occasional memory lapses. While these changes are expected, they can cause concern. When does forgetfulness or slowed thinking indicate the early stages of something more serious?

In this chapter, we will cover the typical cognitive changes that occur with aging and explain how they differ from the cognitive decline associated with dementia. By understanding these differences, you will be able to recognize which changes are part of normal aging and which may require further attention. This knowledge can provide reassurance and help determine when concerns about cognitive function may warrant a medical evaluation.

Normal Aging

Aging is a continuous process that affects both the body and the mind. While certain cognitive and physical changes are inevitable, they are generally mild and do not interfere with a person's ability to function in daily life. Below are some common aspects of normal aging that individuals may experience as they grow older.

Cognitive Slowing

As the brain ages, it processes information more slowly. Older adults may take longer to make quick decisions or complete mental calculations, but their ability to think critically and logically remains intact. Problem-solving may require more time, but this shift reflects a more deliberate and careful approach rather than a decline in cognitive ability.

Aging can also affect focus. Many older adults find it harder to concentrate for long periods, especially in noisy or distracting environments. They may need more frequent breaks or prefer quieter settings to maintain attention and complete tasks efficiently.

Learning new skills or absorbing new information takes more time and repetition with age. However, older adults can still acquire new knowledge and adapt to changes with practice and patience. The ability to adapt to new technologies, concepts, or hobbies remains possible, even though it requires more effort than in younger years.

As people age, they often notice that recalling information takes longer or that memories do not surface as easily as before. For example, forgetting a name or an appointment for a short time is common, but the memory usually returns within minutes or hours. These temporary lapses do not interfere significantly with daily life and differ from the severe memory loss seen in dementia, where entire events or conversations may disappear from recall altogether (National Institute on Aging, 2023a).

Many older adults experience the "tip-of-the-tongue" phenomenon, where a familiar word or name feels just out of reach. Although they recognize that they know the word, they struggle to retrieve it immediately. While this experience can be frustrating, it remains a normal part of aging. It reflects a slowing in the brain's processing speed rather than a loss of vocabulary or verbal ability.

Some older adults develop mild cognitive impairment (MCI), a condition that causes more noticeable memory or thinking difficulties than expected for their age. Despite these challenges, most individuals with MCI continue managing their daily responsibilities and maintaining independence. Approximately 12% to 16% of people over 60 are living with MCI (Alzheimer's Association, 2022).

Understanding the potential progression of MCI to dementia is an important aspect of managing your cognitive health. Statistically, about 10% to 15% of people with MCI progress to Alzheimer's disease each year (Alzheimer's Association, 2022). This rate is notably higher compared to the general population, where only 1% to 2% progress to dementia annually. However, it's important to remember that MCI doesn't always lead to dementia. In fact, some individuals with MCI remain stable or even improve over time, especially with supportive interventions and lifestyle changes.

Sensory Changes

Aging also affects the senses, with vision and hearing among the most noticeably impacted. By age 65, about one-third of older adults experience some level of vision impairment, and by 75, nearly half develop disabling hearing loss (National Institute on Aging, 2023b). Many also experience anosmia, which is a reduced sense of smell. These sensory changes can slow information processing because the brain receives weaker sensory input. For example, a noisy room may make conversations harder to follow due to hearing loss and the brain's reduced ability to filter out background noise.

Losing senses like vision, hearing, and smell can significantly influence cognitive decline. Vision impairment affects everyday activities such as reading, driving, and exercising, leading to reduced mobility, emotional strain, and social withdrawal—all factors that increase dementia risk. Experts estimate that treating vision loss could have prevented tens of thousands of dementia cases in the U.S. (National Institute on Aging, 2023b).

In 2022, two significant studies explored the link between dementia and vision problems, shedding light on how eye health might relate to cognitive decline. Cao et al. (2022) conducted a meta-analysis of 16 studies, suggesting that vision impairment, particularly cataracts and eye issues linked to diabetes, often appears before dementia onset. These visual conditions could act as early warning signs for cognitive decline. Shang et al. (2021) used UK Biobank data to identify eye conditions, such as age-related macular degeneration, cataracts, and diabetes-related eye diseases, as risk factors for Alzheimer's disease. Glaucoma, however, correlated with vascular dementia rather than Alzheimer's. The study also found that the link between vision problems and dementia was stronger in individuals with other health issues like cardiovascular disease or type 2 diabetes, highlighting the role of systemic health in this relationship.

The traditional explanation for the correlation between dementia and vision problems is that both are simply part of the aging process. Dementia is commonly attributed to irreversible brain changes, while age-related vision issues, like macular degeneration, are considered natural developments as people age. However, this view does not fully address the connections observed between vision problems and dementia (Assil, 2022).

Another possible explanation is that vision impairment may exacerbate dementia's progression. Issues such as peripheral vision loss, poor depth perception, and blurred visual clarity can worsen confusion and cognitive decline, which are early indicators of Alzheimer's disease. Individuals with vision problems may struggle to recognize faces, navigate familiar environments, or retain new information, which can significantly impair their ability to function independently, thus accelerating dementia-related challenges.

Dr. Nathaniel Chin, a geriatric specialist, suggests that vision loss might hasten cognitive decline. He argues that vision loss reduces sensory input to the brain, which could contribute to the breakdown of cognitive processes. The brain thrives on sensory stimulation, and the lack of visual input can impair functions like problem-solving and reasoning, potentially accelerating dementia progression (Assil, 2022).

Alternatively, it's also plausible that dementia itself causes vision problems. In certain types of dementia, such as dementia with Lewy bodies, abnormal protein deposits accumulate in the brain regions responsible for visual processing. This can lead to symptoms such as blurry vision, trouble judging distances, and difficulty perceiving colors, even when the eyes themselves are healthy. This suggests that cognitive decline directly impacts visual processing in these cases, making diagnosis and treatment more challenging (Assil, 2022).

In summary, the research indicates a two-way relationship between dementia and vision loss, where vision problems may speed up dementia progression, and brain changes associated with dementia can aggravate vision impairments.

Hearing loss contributes to cognitive decline in similar ways. When the brain struggles to process unclear sounds, it diverts mental resources from memory and thinking to compensate, creating a cognitive load. People with untreated hearing loss often withdraw from social interactions to avoid the frustration of miscommunication, which reduces the mental stimulation needed to keep the brain active. Research consistently shows that using hearing aids or other treatments for hearing loss may help slow cognitive decline (National Institute on Aging, 2023b).

Smell also plays a key role in brain health because it directly connects to memory-related brain regions. A declining sense of smell has emerged as an early warning sign for neurodegenerative diseases like Alzheimer's. Studies indicate that people with reduced smell sensitivity often show early brain changes linked to dementia (National Institute on Aging, 2023b).

Losing multiple senses—such as vision, hearing, and smell—raises the risk of dementia even further, nearly doubling the likelihood compared to losing just one sense (National Institute on Aging, 2023b). If you or a loved one experiences sensory difficulties, regular check-ups and proper treatment can help manage sensory loss and support long-term cognitive health.

As we discussed in Chapter 1, dementia describes a group of cognitive disorders that cause a significant decline in mental abilities and interfere with daily life. Symptoms vary across different disorders and from person to person. However, unlike normal aging, dementia leads to a more severe and progressive deterioration in brain function. It affects memory, language, problem-solving, behavior, and cognitive skills.

Memory Impairment

Many older adults experience some memory impairment, but dementia causes severe forgetfulness. Individuals with dementia often forget recent events or conversations and typically do not recall them later. They may repeatedly ask for the same information or tell the same story multiple times within a short period.

People with dementia frequently become disoriented, even in familiar settings. They may get lost in places they have visited many times, such as their neighborhood or home. In more severe cases, they might forget how they arrived at a location or struggle to follow basic directions. Confusion about time and place indicates cognitive decline beyond what occurs with normal aging (Alzheimer's Association, 2024).

Cognitive Decline

Dementia disrupts problem-solving and planning abilities. Tasks that require step-by-step thinking, such as following a recipe or managing finances, become increasingly difficult. For example, someone with dementia may struggle to follow the steps of a simple recipe they have cooked for years or have difficulty paying bills. As dementia progresses, individuals eventually lose the ability to manage their own affairs (Alzheimer's Association, 2024).

Dementia also weakens decision-making skills, leading to risky or irresponsible behaviors. Individuals may give away large sums of money to strangers, fall victim to scams, or neglect personal hygiene and health. Their choices may endanger their safety and well-being. For instance, they might leave home inadequately dressed for the weather or attempt to drive when it is no longer safe. Unlike normal aging, where decision-making slows but remains mostly reliable, dementia causes a significant decline in judgment.

Language and Communication

Dementia also severely affects language abilities. When struggling to find the right words, individuals may replace specific nouns with vague terms like "thing" or "it." They may also find it difficult to join conversations or follow discussions. While normal aging may cause occasional word-finding problems, it does not disrupt communication to the same extent.

In advanced stages, speech may become incoherent or nonsensical. Individuals might jumble words together or form sentences that do not make sense. Language processing abilities decline significantly, a pattern not seen in normal aging. Over time, severe dementia can lead to the complete loss of verbal communication (Alzheimer's Association, 2024).

Behavioral Changes

Dementia causes drastic mood swings. Individuals may suddenly feel confused, suspicious, anxious, or depressed, even in situations that previously did not provoke such emotions. They might accuse loved ones of stealing, experience paranoia, or become upset without an apparent trigger. These emotional shifts go beyond the occasional frustration or irritability that can accompany normal aging.

Dementia may also alter personality. Previously social individuals may withdraw from interactions, while others may behave rudely or inappropriately in public, even if they never acted that way before. As dementia affects the brain regions responsible for social behavior and emotional regulation, individuals may display unpredictable or unusual behaviors (Alzheimer's Association, 2024).

In summary, normal aging brings mild cognitive and physical changes, such as slower memory recall and reduced processing speed, without significantly affecting daily life. In contrast, dementia causes severe and progressive impairments, including frequent memory loss, noticeable cognitive decline, and noticeable behavioral or personality changes that disrupt daily functioning.

Self Assessment

Self-assessment can be a helpful first step in understanding where you stand. I recommend using a cognitive self-assessment questionnaire. These tools, available online and in some healthcare settings, allow you to evaluate your memory, reasoning, and other cognitive functions from home. They're designed to be straightforward and can provide a baseline of your cognitive health. Digital tools are also becoming more popular. Apps and software that track cognitive performance over time can offer insights into your brain health. They might include games that test memory or puzzles that challenge your problem-solving skills. The key is to use these tools regularly and track your results. If you notice significant changes or areas where you consistently struggle, it might be time to consult a professional.

Here are 13 free self-assessments that you can use to evaluate your cognitive health today:

1. BCAT Self-Assessment Tools
2. BCRS, FAST, and GDS
3. Brief Evaluation of Executive Function
4. Dementia Severity Rating Scale
5. Functional Activities Questionnaire
6. IQCODE
7. Lawton-Brody IADL
8. Mini MoCA Self Screen
9. Neuro-QoL
10. SAGE
11. Short Blessed Test
12. SLUMS
13. Iowa Trail Making Test (Young, 2018).

If you do decide to seek professional evaluation, start by documenting any cognitive changes you've noticed. Keep a journal or list of instances when memory lapses or confusion have impacted your life. This record will help your healthcare provider understand your situation better. During the consultation, don't hesitate to discuss your concerns openly. Your healthcare provider is there to help, and they need a complete picture to make accurate assessments. They might suggest further tests or evaluations to pinpoint the issue. Remember, early intervention can make a significant difference in managing cognitive health.

By understanding the difference between normal aging and potential cognitive issues, you empower yourself to take control of your brain health. Taking proactive steps, whether through self-assessment or professional consultation, can help you navigate the changes that come with aging more effectively. This approach supports your cognitive well-being and enhances your overall health and independence as you age. As we continue to explore the complexities of cognitive health, being informed and proactive remains your best defense against the challenges that aging can bring.

Chapter 3

Early Detection and Diagnosis

The early detection and diagnosis of dementia is integral to providing patients with the best possible care and treatment options. In this chapter, we'll explore different detection methods, including the analysis of biomarkers, brain imaging, blood tests, and cerebrospinal fluid. We will also explore how AI is revolutionizing and improving our ability to detect dementia early.

Biomarkers

The current approach to diagnosing Alzheimer's disease relies primarily on identifying cognitive decline, a stage where significant brain damage has already occurred (Alzheimer's Association, n.d.). This limitation highlights the urgent need for methods that can detect Alzheimer's earlier, ideally before symptoms begin to affect daily life. Researchers believe that biomarkers—measurable biological indicators—offer a promising avenue for earlier detection. Think of biomarkers as the body's way of sending out signals, like an early warning system. They provide insights into pathological changes that occur before symptoms even appear, allowing for timely interventions.

In the context of dementia, biomarkers help identify changes in the brain that might not yet be noticeable through cognitive tests or physical symptoms. These markers can include proteins, genes, or other molecules that signal disease processes. In recent years, advancements in biomarker research have opened new avenues for detecting dementia early, offering hope for more effective management and treatment strategies. Identifying reliable biomarkers for Alzheimer's would improve early diagnosis and intervention, potentially slowing disease progression.

Several promising biomarkers are under investigation, including changes in beta-amyloid and tau protein levels in cerebrospinal fluid (CSF) and structural and functional brain changes visible through imaging techniques. Research suggests that these indicators evolve at different stages of the disease, providing a timeline of disease progression.

For a biomarker to be used in clinical settings, it must undergo rigorous validation. Researchers must demonstrate that the biomarker consistently and accurately indicates the presence of Alzheimer's across diverse populations. Additionally, laboratory methods used to measure these biomarkers must be standardized to ensure reliability.

Currently, the U.S. Food and Drug Administration (FDA) has approved some diagnostic tools, such as brain imaging techniques, for individuals showing symptoms of Alzheimer's or other dementias. While some of these tools, like CSF biomarkers, are already supported by extensive research, others, such as blood tests and genetic risk profiling, are still in development. As scientific understanding advances, these emerging diagnostic methods may become crucial for routine Alzheimer's screening (Alzheimer's Association, n.d.).

Brain Imaging

Brain imaging plays a key role in detecting Alzheimer's, with ongoing research focusing on improving imaging techniques to detect the disease earlier and with greater accuracy. Different types of imaging provide valuable information about the brain's structure, function, and chemical composition.

Structural Imaging

Structural imaging assesses the shape, position, and volume of brain tissue. Magnetic resonance imaging (MRI) and computed tomography (CT) scans fall into this category. These techniques have shown that the brains of individuals with Alzheimer's shrink significantly as the disease progresses. Research indicates that shrinkage in specific areas, such as the hippocampus, may be one of the earliest signs of the disease. Standardized measurements of brain volume loss are becoming increasingly useful in diagnosing Alzheimer's and monitoring its progression.

In clinical practice, structural imaging is often used to rule out other conditions that mimic Alzheimer's symptoms, such as strokes, tumors, severe head trauma, or fluid accumulation in the brain. These scans help ensure that individuals receive appropriate treatment for their specific condition (Alzheimer's Association, n.d.).

Functional Imaging

Functional imaging examines how different brain regions operate by measuring how actively brain cells consume glucose or oxygen. This category includes positron emission tomography (PET) and functional MRI (fMRI). Studies using fluorodeoxyglucose (FDG)-PET scans show that individuals with Alzheimer's typically have reduced glucose metabolism in brain areas responsible for memory, learning, and problem-solving.

According to Medicare guidelines, FDG-PET scans are recommended for individuals with recent dementia diagnoses and at least six months of documented cognitive decline when both Alzheimer's and frontotemporal dementia are suspected. This imaging technique can help differentiate between types of dementia, leading to more targeted treatment strategies (Alzheimer's Association, n.d.).

Molecular Imaging

Molecular imaging, another form of PET scanning, is one of the most active areas of Alzheimer's research. This technique uses radiotracers to detect biological changes associated with the disease before structural or functional damage occurs.

Molecular imaging could allow for earlier diagnosis, better disease monitoring, and improved assessment of new treatments designed to modify disease progression.

Several molecular imaging compounds have been studied, and four have been approved for clinical use:

- **Florbetaben (Neuraceq®), Florbetapir (Amyvid®), and Flutemetamol (Vizamyl®):** These tracers detect beta-amyloid plaques in the brain.
- **Flortaucipir F18 (Tauvid®):** This tracer detects tau protein tangles in the brain (Alzheimer's Association, n.d.).

Remember, while the presence of amyloid plaques is a hallmark of Alzheimer's, it is not sufficient for diagnosis on its own. Physicians must evaluate multiple factors, including cognitive assessments, laboratory tests, and imaging results, to confirm an Alzheimer's diagnosis or rule out other causes of cognitive impairment.

Limitations

Despite their benefits, these imaging techniques come with challenges that limit their routine clinical use. The high cost of PET and MRI scans can be prohibitive, often making them inaccessible to many patients without comprehensive insurance coverage. Additionally, the availability of advanced imaging equipment is not uniform across healthcare settings, with many facilities lacking the resources to offer these scans. Furthermore, the interpretation of imaging results requires specialized training and expertise, which can be a barrier in areas with limited access to skilled radiologists. These factors combine to create a situation where, despite their diagnostic potential, advanced imaging techniques are not yet a staple in everyday dementia care.

The limitations in accessibility highlight the need for ongoing research and development to reduce costs and improve availability. Innovations in imaging technology could pave the way for more widespread use, bringing these powerful diagnostic tools to a broader patient population. As the technology evolves, there is hope that imaging will become a routine part of dementia diagnosis, offering detailed insights that can guide treatment decisions and improve patient outcomes. The integration of imaging with other diagnostic methods, such as cognitive assessments and biomarkers, holds the promise of a more holistic approach to dementia care. This synergy could lead to earlier detection, more accurate diagnoses, and ultimately, better-targeted therapies that address the specific needs of each patient.

Blood Tests

Blood-based biomarkers are an area of intense research, as they could offer a simple, non-invasive, and cost-effective method for early Alzheimer's detection. Scientists are studying whether changes in tau, beta-amyloid, or other markers in the blood can reliably indicate disease progression.

Blood tests have the potential to support drug development by identifying individuals who would benefit from early intervention and monitoring treatment effectiveness. Additionally, these tests could help researchers understand Alzheimer's progression across different populations.

Currently, some blood tests are available for use by specialists treating individuals with memory complaints, though none have FDA approval. These tests may predict the presence of amyloid plaques or neurodegenerative damage, but they cannot yet serve as stand-alone diagnostic tools. Instead, they are used alongside other medical evaluations to assess cognitive decline (Alzheimer's Association, n.d.).

Among the cutting-edge developments in this field is the PrecivityAD test. This blood test is designed to aid in the diagnosis of Alzheimer's disease, particularly for individuals aged 60 and older experiencing cognitive impairment. It uses advanced mass spectrometry techniques to measure the concentration ratio of two amyloid-beta peptides, Abeta 42 and 40, while also detecting the APOE genotype. These markers help determine the likelihood of Alzheimer's disease, providing an Amyloid Probability Score (APS) that predicts the presence of amyloid plaques in the brain. A high APS suggests a greater likelihood of Alzheimer's, offering a valuable tool for early intervention.

The PrecivityAD test also reduces the need for amyloid PET imaging, which, while effective, involves radiation exposure and higher costs. At $1,250, the PrecivityAD test is more affordable than PET scans, making it a viable option for wider accessibility. Despite its promise, the test isn't without limitations. Factors like chronic kidney disease and obesity may affect its accuracy, and further research is needed to establish its role in improving clinical outcomes (Alzheimer's Association, n.d.).

Cerebrospinal Fluid (CSF) Tests

CSF is a clear fluid that surrounds the brain and spinal cord, serving as a protective cushion. Physicians can collect CSF samples through a lumbar puncture (spinal tap), a minimally invasive procedure. Research suggests that Alzheimer's disease causes changes in CSF levels of beta-amyloid and tau, two proteins that form abnormal deposits in the brain.

Another promising biomarker in CSF is neurofilament light (NfL), a protein that increases in neurodegenerative diseases like Alzheimer's. One challenge in using CSF biomarkers is ensuring consistency in measurements across different laboratories and testing platforms. However, efforts to standardize these measurements have significantly improved their reliability.

The FDA has approved the Lumipulse® CSF Amyloid Ratio test, which can detect amyloid changes predictive of Alzheimer's. The Alzheimer's Association has also established guidelines to promote the safe and appropriate use of CSF testing in clinical practice (Alzheimer's Association, n.d.).

Genetic Risk Profiling

As we discussed in Chapter 1, scientists have identified multiple genes associated with Alzheimer's. Some rare genetic mutations, such as those in the APP, PSEN1, and PSEN2 genes, directly cause inherited forms of the disease, known as dominantly inherited Alzheimer's disease. However, most cases of Alzheimer's are not directly inherited but influenced by genetic risk factors.

The APOE-e4 gene variant is the strongest known genetic risk factor for late-onset Alzheimer's, though carrying this variant does not guarantee that an individual will develop the disease. Researchers continue to investigate additional genes that may contribute to Alzheimer's risk or offer protection against it.

Genetic testing for Alzheimer's risk is currently used in some clinical trials to identify participants who may respond to experimental treatments. As more targeted therapies become available, genetic profiling may play a larger role in personalized risk assessment and treatment planning (Alzheimer's Association, n.d.).

AI in Diagnosis

In dementia diagnosis, AI offers groundbreaking potential. AI algorithms excel at pattern recognition, processing vast amounts of cognitive data to identify subtle changes that might signal the onset of dementia. This capability is especially promising in the early stages, where traditional diagnostic methods might miss critical signs. By learning from a wide array of data inputs, machine learning models can predict how the disease might progress, offering a proactive approach to treatment and care planning.

A 2021 study from Grueso and Viejo-Sobera states that Cambridge scientists have developed an artificially intelligent tool capable of predicting in four cases out of five whether people with early signs of dementia will remain stable or develop Alzheimer's disease. The machine learning model is able to predict whether and how fast an individual with mild memory and thinking problems will progress to developing Alzheimer's disease.

The algorithm was able to distinguish between people with stable mild cognitive impairment and those who progressed to Alzheimer's disease within a three-year period. It was able to correctly identify individuals who went on to develop Alzheimer's in 82% of cases and correctly identify those who didn't in 81% of cases from cognitive tests and an MRI scan alone.

The algorithm was around three times more accurate at predicting the progression to Alzheimer's than the current standard of care, which is standard clinical markers (such as grey matter atrophy or cognitive scores) or clinical diagnosis. This shows that the model could significantly reduce misdiagnosis.

Senior author Professor Zoe Kourtzi from the Department of Psychology at the University of Cambridge said, "We've created a tool which, despite using only data from cognitive tests and MRI scans, is much more sensitive than current approaches at predicting whether someone will progress from mild symptoms to Alzheimer's—and if so, whether this progress will be fast or slow.

"This has the potential to significantly improve patient well-being, showing us which people need closest care, while removing the anxiety for those patients we predict will remain stable. At a time of intense pressure on healthcare resources, this will also help remove the need for unnecessary invasive and costly diagnostic tests" (Grueso & Viejo-Sobera, 2021).

Montreal Cognitive Assessment

One tool that has significantly benefited from AI advancements is the Montreal Cognitive Assessment (MOCA). MOCA is a widely used screening tool designed to detect mild cognitive impairment. Traditionally, its effectiveness depended heavily on the skill and experience of the individual administering the test. However, with AI enhancements, the accuracy and efficiency of MOCA have improved substantially.

In 2023, Mila, the world's largest academic deep learning research center based in Quebec, formed a partnership with MoCA Cognition, the company behind the leading test for early detection of cognitive impairment. The collaboration will focus on applying AI models to digital cognitive assessments, primarily aimed at identifying Alzheimer's disease and dementia (MOCA Cognition, 2023).

AI can assist in scoring and interpreting MOCA results, reducing human error and providing more consistent assessments. By integrating AI with MOCA, healthcare professionals can combine it with other cognitive assessment tools, offering a comprehensive analysis of an individual's cognitive health. This integration allows for a multi-faceted approach to diagnosis, capturing a broader spectrum of cognitive function and potential decline.

Eye-Alzheimer's

Researchers are also using AI in other ways. A study from Hao et al. in 2024 explained the development of Eye-Alzheimer's, a deep learning model designed to detect early-onset Alzheimer's disease and mild cognitive impairment (MCI) using optical coherence tomography angiography images. In more simple terms, Eye-Alzheimer's uses a multilevel graph approach to analyze retinal images, focusing on both small and large blood vessels in the retina.

The study analyzed retinal imaging data from 1,671 participants, making it one of the largest datasets used for early-onset Alzheimer's and MCI detection. The results emphasize the importance of the eye's blood vessels as a biomarker for early-stage dementia. However, the study's sample size limits its generalizability, particularly in terms of ethnic diversity, highlighting the need for more diverse and larger cohorts (Hao et al., 2024).

Importantly, Eye-Alzheimer's shows promise as a non-invasive method for detecting Alzheimer's and MCI, potentially improving early diagnosis and treatment.

AI's role in dementia diagnosis is a testament to how technology can reshape our approach to medical care. By enhancing tools like

MOCA and introducing new digital platforms, AI enables earlier, more accurate detection of cognitive decline.

In summary, the combination of biomarkers, brain imaging, blood tests, genetic profiling, and AI are transforming the way dementia is diagnosed, offering more accurate and earlier identification of the disease. As we look ahead, it is equally important to explore strategies for preventing dementia. The next chapter will focus on lifestyle factors and interventions that can potentially reduce the risk of developing dementia.

Chapter 4
Lifestyle Interventions for Prevention

In this chapter, we will explore strategies to prevent dementia by building cognitive reserve—the brain's ability to adapt and withstand damage. Research suggests that engaging in mentally stimulating activities, staying physically active, and following a brain-healthy diet can all contribute to preserving cognitive function as we age. Cognitive reserve acts as a protective buffer, enabling the brain to compensate for damage that may occur over time. With these combined efforts, we can strengthen our cognitive reserve and reduce the risk of dementia-related decline.

Neuroplasticity and Cognitive Reserve

Neuroplasticity, the brain's ability to reorganize and form new neural connections, plays a central role in maintaining cognitive resilience, especially as we age. This process allows the brain to adapt to new experiences, learning, and thought patterns by adjusting its structure and function. Although neuroplasticity is most pronounced during childhood, where it supports the development of language, motor skills, and cognitive abilities, recent research has demonstrated that this adaptability persists throughout adulthood (Ackerman, 2018). The brain's ability to undergo structural and functional changes offers new possibilities for recovery, adaptation, and resilience in the face of cognitive challenges, including neurodegenerative diseases like dementia.

Neuroplasticity can be classified into two main types: functional plasticity and structural plasticity. Functional plasticity enables the brain to shift functions from damaged or inactive areas to healthier regions. This process is especially evident when certain brain regions are impaired, such as in the aftermath of a stroke or brain injury, where other areas compensate for lost functions (Ness Care Group, 2022). On the other hand, structural plasticity involves the brain physically reorganizing itself by creating new neural pathways or strengthening existing ones. Repeated learning and engagement can reshape the brain, making it more efficient in supporting cognitive processes like memory and attention (Ackerman, 2018).

The concept of neuroplasticity is particularly significant when discussing cognitive resilience in individuals affected by dementia. Diseases like Alzheimer's and vascular dementia lead to the degeneration of neural pathways, which can severely impair memory, learning, and other cognitive functions. Amyloid plaques, tau tangles, and inflammation disrupt the brain's ability to form new synapses (Ness Care Group, 2022). These disruptions undermine synaptic plasticity, hindering the brain's capacity for learning and adaptation. Despite these challenges, research indicates that certain areas of the brain, like the prefrontal cortex, may retain neuroplasticity even in individuals with dementia. This remaining plasticity suggests that cognitive functions may still be preserved or restored if targeted interventions are employed in a timely manner (Ness Care Group, 2022).

The remaining neuroplasticity in the brain of individuals with dementia is closely tied to the concept of cognitive reserve. Cognitive reserve refers to the brain's ability to tolerate damage and continue functioning effectively. Those with higher cognitive reserves may have more neurons or neural connections to take over functions from damaged areas, allowing them to retain cognitive abilities even in the face of neurodegenerative processes. The development of cognitive reserve is influenced by a lifetime of intellectual and social engagement, including education, mentally stimulating occupations, and a rich social life. As we mentioned in Chapter 1, these are all modifiable risk factors believed to increase the risk of dementia. Though cognitive reserve does not prevent dementia entirely, it may delay the onset of symptoms or slow the progression of the disease (Ness Care Group, 2022). This resilience highlights the importance of maintaining cognitive engagement throughout life, as a well-stimulated brain is better equipped to withstand the effects of aging and pathology.

A study by Edwards et al. (2017) further reinforces the link between neuroplasticity and cognitive reserve. Their research demonstrated that brain training exercises, such as speed-of-processing training, could reduce the risk of dementia by enhancing neural pathways associated with cognitive processing. Over a 10-year follow-up period, participants who engaged in this training had a 29% lower risk of developing dementia compared to the control group. The study's findings align with the broader understanding of neuroplasticity, emphasizing that cognitive engagement—through activities like problem-solving, learning new skills, or engaging in cognitive games—can help maintain or even improve cognitive functions by promoting the brain's ability to adapt and form new connections (Edwards et al., 2017).

Aging and neurodegenerative diseases like dementia may challenge the brain's ability to adapt, but evidence suggests that specific lifestyle choices can support neuroplasticity and help maintain cognitive function. Physical activity, mental stimulation, and nutrition are three lifestyle factors that have been shown to positively influence neuroplasticity, particularly in older adults.

Physical Activity

Physical activity is one of the most widely recognized factors influencing brain health and neuroplasticity. Research consistently shows that regular physical activity enhances cognitive performance, including memory, attention, and problem-solving abilities. Beyond just improving fitness, engaging in physical exercise has a profound effect on the brain, promoting various beneficial processes that support neuroplasticity.

A growing body of evidence highlights that regular physical activity, particularly aerobic exercise, can slow down age-related brain decline and reduce the risk of cognitive impairments such as dementia. Studies have shown that adults who are active during midlife tend to experience less cognitive decline as they age compared to those who lead sedentary lifestyles (Phillips, 2017). For example, a longitudinal study over 26 years found that individuals who engaged in physical exercise had better memory retention and faster processing speeds as they entered older adulthood (Phillips, 2017).

Physical activity has several mechanisms by which it promotes neuroplasticity. One of the most notable is neurogenesis—the formation of new neurons. Exercise stimulates the release of brain-derived neurotrophic factor (BDNF), a protein that supports the growth and survival of neurons. BDNF is especially important in brain regions involved in memory and learning, such as the hippocampus. As BDNF levels increase with physical activity, the brain is better able to form new synapses and retain cognitive function.

In addition to neurogenesis, exercise also improves the brain's antioxidant defense mechanisms, which help protect against oxidative stress, a contributor to cognitive decline. When we exercise, the body produces fewer free radicals, which are molecules that can damage cells, including brain cells. Regular physical activity, particularly aerobic exercises like walking, running, or cycling, also improves cardiovascular health, ensuring that the brain receives an adequate supply of oxygen and nutrients. Studies indicate that those who maintain a higher level of cardiovascular fitness show preserved cortical tissue density, particularly in regions essential for executive function, such as the frontal and temporal lobes (Phillips, 2017).

Moreover, exercise reduces inflammation, which is an important factor in the aging brain. Chronic inflammation can negatively impact brain function and lead to neurodegenerative diseases (Phillips, 2017). Regular physical activity can help regulate the body's inflammatory responses, keeping them at healthier levels and potentially preventing the development of cognitive disorders like Alzheimer's disease.

Mental Stimulation

Mental stimulation is another important factor that can promote neuroplasticity and cognitive health. Engaging in intellectually challenging activities encourages the brain to form new connections and strengthen existing ones. Mental engagement supports the concept of cognitive reserve, which refers to the brain's ability to tolerate damage or pathology without showing clinical signs of cognitive decline. Cognitive reserve is built up through years of engaging in mentally stimulating activities, such as learning new skills, solving puzzles, or reading.

Individuals who maintain an active and engaged mind are less likely to experience significant cognitive decline, even when they have brain pathology associated with Alzheimer's or other dementias. Studies have shown that people with higher cognitive reserve tend to exhibit less pronounced cognitive symptoms despite having the same amount of brain damage as those with lower cognitive reserve (Alzheimer's Association, 2024). Activities that challenge the brain, such as solving complex problems, learning new languages, or participating in intellectually demanding hobbies, help to build and maintain cognitive reserve, making the brain more resilient to damage.

Social engagement is another aspect of mental stimulation. Regular social interaction both promotes emotional well-being and stimulates cognitive processes. Interacting with others requires the brain to process information, remember details, and engage in meaningful conversations, all of which help maintain cognitive abilities. Studies have shown that people who maintain strong social networks and engage in regular social activities, such as participating in clubs, attending family gatherings, or volunteering, have a reduced risk of dementia and other cognitive impairments (Phillips, 2017). Socializing provides a mental workout and helps to keep the brain agile, thus supporting neuroplasticity.

Nutrition

Diet also has an essential role in maintaining brain health and supporting neuroplasticity, particularly as we age. The brain requires a significant amount of energy to carry out its complex functions, and poor nutrition can hinder its ability to function optimally. Research has shown that diets rich in specific nutrients can support cognitive function and protect against neurodegenerative diseases like Alzheimer's (Phillips, 2017).

One of the most well-researched nutrients for brain health is omega-3 fatty acids, which are found in foods like fatty fish, flaxseeds, walnuts, and chia seeds. Omega-3 fatty acids are essential for maintaining the structure of brain cells and supporting synaptic plasticity—the ability of synapses to strengthen or weaken over time. Synaptic plasticity is necessary for learning and memory formation. Studies have shown that a diet rich in omega-3 fatty acids can improve cognitive function, particularly in areas related to memory and learning (Phillips, 2017). Furthermore, omega-3 fatty acids have anti-inflammatory properties, which help protect the brain from damage caused by chronic inflammation.

Studies in mice have shown that DHA (docosahexaenoic acid), an omega-3 fatty acid found in salmon, reduced beta-amyloid plaques. However, human trials have produced mixed results. One study with 485 older adults showed that taking DHA daily for 24 weeks improved learning and memory. In contrast, a study of

4,000 adults did not find omega-3 supplements helped slow cognitive decline (National Institute on Aging, 2023c).

Polyphenols, which are abundant in fruits, vegetables, tea, and dark chocolate, also play an important role in supporting cognitive health. These antioxidants help protect the brain from oxidative stress. Polyphenols have been shown to improve cognitive function and may also help reduce the risk of developing dementia (Phillips, 2017).

In addition to these beneficial compounds, a balanced diet that includes a variety of fruits, vegetables, whole grains, and lean proteins is essential for overall brain health. Nutrients such as vitamins B, C, D, and E, as well as minerals like magnesium and zinc, are all needed for cognitive function. These vitamins and minerals support neural health by promoting energy production, protecting against oxidative damage, and supporting neurotransmitter function.

Currently, no specific vitamin or supplement is recommended to prevent Alzheimer's. However, a 2023 study found that multivitamins improved memory test scores in older adults compared to a placebo. Additionally, a 2022 study showed that those who took a daily multivitamin performed better on cognitive tests and showed significant improvements in memory and executive function compared to those who did not take one (National Institute on Aging, 2023c).

On the other hand, diets that are high in processed sugars, trans fats, and refined carbohydrates have been shown to have negative effects on brain health. High sugar intake can impair insulin function, leading to inflammation and the disruption of brain signaling pathways. Processed fats, such as trans fats found in fast food and baked goods, can contribute to the development of plaque in the brain, a hallmark of Alzheimer's disease. These dietary patterns impair neuroplasticity and are associated with cognitive deficits, particularly in memory and learning (Phillips, 2017).

Diet might also indirectly affect Alzheimer's risk factors like diabetes, obesity, and heart disease. For example, the typical Western diet, which is high in red meat and saturated fats, may increase the risk of cardiovascular disease, potentially speeding up brain aging (National Institute on Aging, 2023c). A growing area of research examines the role of gut microbes—microorganisms in the digestive system—and their connection to aging processes that lead to Alzheimer's. We will explore this further in Chapter 11.

There are some diets that are believed to be linked to a lower risk of dementia compared to a typical Western diet.

The Mediterranean and Mind Diets

The Mediterranean diet focuses on fruits, vegetables, whole grains, legumes, fish, unsaturated fats like olive oil, and limited amounts of red meat, eggs, and sweets. The MIND diet combines elements of the Mediterranean and DASH (Dietary Approaches to Stop Hypertension) diets. The MIND diet features vegetables, especially leafy greens, berries, whole grains, beans, nuts, fish, and olive oil, while limiting red meat, sweets, cheese, butter, and fried foods.

Previous research suggests these diets may slow cognitive decline, reduce dementia risk, and lower brain damage. In March 2023, scientists examined the brains of around 600 older adults who died at an average age of 91. Autopsies showed that those who adhered to the Mediterranean or MIND diet had fewer signs of Alzheimer's pathologies, such as tau tangles and amyloid plaques. In another study, researchers found that, after 4.5 years, people most consistent with the MIND diet experienced a 53% slower rate of Alzheimer's compared to those who did not follow it closely (National Institute on Aging, 2023c).

However, a recent clinical trial with 600 older adults, all with a family history of dementia, tested the MIND diet against a control diet. Results showed only modest cognitive improvements in those following the MIND diet, similar to those in the control group (National Institute on Aging, 2023c).

In this chapter, we covered the importance of building cognitive reserve through mental stimulation, physical exercise, and a brain-healthy diet as a means of preventing dementia. These strategies offer practical ways to protect our brain health, potentially delaying or reducing the onset of dementia. However, while these preventive measures are useful tools, they are not foolproof. As we move forward, it is essential that we explore the latest advancements in dementia treatment. In the next chapter, we will examine recent breakthroughs in medical research and treatment approaches that aim to slow or even reverse the effects of dementia, providing hope for those affected and their families.

Spreading Awareness

"In fair weather, prepare for foul."

— Thomas Fuller

As you may remember from the beginning of the book, the number of Americans over the age of 65 living with Alzheimer's is expected to rise to almost 13 million in the next 25 years. That's nearly double what it is today. Having seen through my work how dementia affects many families of all kinds, it's become very clear to me that everyone needs to know more about it. There's a chance it could affect any one of us, whether directly or because a loved one develops it. We need to be prepared for this possibility. We need to know what we can do to protect our own cognitive health, and we need to understand more about the condition we're dealing with to advocate for those we love.

My passion for sharing this information comes both from my work as a nurse and from my personal experience with my parents. I count myself lucky that I had my nursing experience to inform my caregiving; this isn't the case for everyone. I'm determined to use my experiences for good and help as many people as I can to feel more prepared to protect against and deal with dementia—and since I already know that this is something that concerns you, I'd like to ask for your help. The best part is, all you have to do to make a real difference is leave a short review.

By leaving a review of this book on Amazon, you'll help it become more visible to others searching for this information.

There are a lot of people who want to understand more about dementia and what they can do to protect their cognitive health or prepare for the possibility that someone they love may eventually develop it. By making resources visible, we can help them to find what they're looking for.

Thank you so much for your support. The number of people who live with dementia is growing—and so, too, must our awareness.

Scan the QR code below.

Chapter 5

Treatment Advances and Emerging Therapies

In this chapter, we will cover the current treatments for Alzheimer's disease, focusing on both symptomatic management and disease-modifying therapies. Alzheimer's disease is a complex, progressive neurodegenerative disorder, and while no cure currently exists, various medications aim to alleviate symptoms and slow the disease's progression. We will explore drugs such as Lecameb and Donaemab, which show promise in targeting underlying disease mechanisms like amyloid plaques. Additionally, we will discuss symptomatic treatments that help improve cognitive function and daily living. Beyond existing therapies, we will also review emerging research areas, including therapeutic plasma exchange, efforts to reduce inflammation in the brain, and other innovative approaches to tackling Alzheimer's at a molecular level. All of these treatments and research directions are representative the ongoing effort to manage and eventually overcome Alzheimer's disease.

FDA-Approved Medications to Treat Alzheimer's

Lecanemab

Lecanemab is a humanized IgG1 monoclonal antibody designed to target protofibrils, which are soluble aggregated forms of amyloid-beta. A humanized IgG1 monoclonal antibody is a type of laboratory-engineered antibody designed to mimic human immune system proteins.

- **Humanized:** The antibody is originally derived from a non-human source (often a mouse) but has been modified to resemble human antibodies, reducing the risk of immune rejection.
- **IgG1:** This refers to a specific subclass of immunoglobulin G (IgG), which is the most common type of antibody in human blood and plays a key role in immune responses.
- **Monoclonal Antibody:** This means it is a single, uniform antibody that targets one specific antigen (in this case, protofibrils of amyloid-beta) (Verga et al., 2023).

In the context of lecanemab, this means the drug is designed to selectively bind to and neutralize amyloid-beta protofibrils, which are implicated in Alzheimer's disease.

The U.S. FDA approved lecanemab for the treatment of Alzheimer's disease on January 6, 2023. This decision was based on a phase 2 clinical trial and supported by results from a phase 3 trial published in November 2022. The phase 3 study involved 1,795 patients with early-stage Alzheimer's, including those with mild cognitive impairment and mild dementia caused by Alzheimer's. This study was the first to demonstrate a significant slowing of disease progression on the clinical dementia rating scale-sum of boxes over 18 months. Patients treated with lecanemab showed a mean change from baseline of -0.45 compared to those receiving a placebo ($p < 0.001$). Additionally, in a subgroup of 698 patients, researchers observed a reduction in amyloid burden through PET imaging in those receiving lecanemab, while those in the placebo group showed no such reduction. An extension study is currently assessing the long-term efficacy, safety, and tolerability of lecanemab, including a sub-study evaluating its subcutaneous administration through amyloid PET monitoring (Verga et al., 2023).

Lecanemab is the second anti-amyloid-beta drug approved by the FDA, following aducanumab. Like lecanemab, aducanumab demonstrated a reduction in amyloid burden on PET scans. However, evidence of its clinical benefits was inconsistent. Only one of two identical phase 3 trials showed a significant slowing of cognitive decline. As a result, aducanumab has not been recommended for clinical use in the United States and has not received approval in Europe. A phase 3b/4 study is underway to determine whether aducanumab provides clinical benefits for early Alzheimer's (Verga et al., 2023).

Unlike aducanumab, lecanemab has consistently shown efficacy across different studies and outcome measures. Researchers attribute this consistency to lecanemab's binding profile. Lecanemab primarily targets amyloid-beta protofibrils, whereas aducanumab and similar monoclonal antibodies focus on highly aggregated forms of amyloid-beta. This difference in targeting may also explain why lecanemab has a lower incidence of amyloid-related imaging abnormalities, such as transient brain swelling (edema) and small brain bleeds (microbleeds), which are associated with immunotherapy (Verga et al., 2023).

Several phase 3 clinical trials are underway or have already been completed for anti-amyloid-beta therapies in early Alzheimer's. These trials have consistently used amyloid PET imaging both as an inclusion criterion and as a secondary endpoint in at least some patients. Another anti-amyloid-beta drug, donanemab, is also undergoing phase 3 trials. Post hoc analyses from its phase 2 trial linked greater amyloid plaque clearance on PET scans with slower tau accumulation and slower cognitive decline in patients carrying the apolipoprotein E ε4 allele. Evidence is growing that anti-amyloid-beta therapies slow cognitive decline in early Alzheimer's (Verga et al., 2023).

Lecanemab is administered intravenously every two weeks, with each infusion lasting approximately one hour. These infusions are typically conducted in hospitals or infusion therapy centers. The manufacturers of lecanemab have set the annual cost of the drug at $26,500. The Centers for Medicare & Medicaid Services has announced that lecanemab will be covered, provided that the prescribing physician enrolls the patient in a CMS-approved registry (Verga et al., 2023).

On January 26, 2025, the FDA approved a maintenance dosing schedule for lecanemab, allowing eligible patients with early Alzheimer's disease to transition to infusions once every four weeks. Patients who have completed the initial 18-month regimen of biweekly infusions may now switch to this less frequent schedule to maintain amyloid clearance in the brain. This decision should be made in consultation with their clinician. The reduced dosing frequency is expected to ease the burden on patients and caregivers, making long-term treatment more manageable (Verga et al., 2023).

Additionally, the drug may soon be even easier to access. The FDA is currently reviewing a new injectable version of lecanemab, which, if approved, would allow patients to self-administer the medication at home using an injector pen—similar to how insulin or Ozempic is delivered. This change could significantly improve accessibility for those who have difficulty traveling to infusion centers. The FDA is expected to make a decision on the at-home injection option by August 2025 (Verga et al., 2023).

Donanemab

Donanemab is a monoclonal antibody therapy that treats early Alzheimer's disease by targeting beta-amyloid plaques in the brain. Beta-amyloid is a protein that accumulates abnormally in Alzheimer's, forming plaques that interfere with brain function and contribute to memory loss and cognitive decline. Donanemab binds to amyloid plaques containing a specific modified form of beta-amyloid called p3+, which is associated with mature plaques. By attaching to these plaques, donanemab activates the immune system to break them down and remove them from the brain. This process helps reduce the amyloid burden, which may slow the progression of the disease (Alzheimer's Association, 2024b).

The treatment is administered once every four weeks through an IV infusion. Unlike some Alzheimer's therapies that require life-long treatment, donanemab follows a "treat-to-clear" approach, meaning that patients may stop receiving infusions once their amyloid levels drop below a specific threshold. This approach aims to provide long-term benefits while minimizing the need for continuous treatment (Alzheimer's Association, 2024b).

Donanemab differs from lecanemab in how it targets amyloid and in its dosing schedule. Lecanemab binds to soluble amyloid protofibrils, which are smaller, early-stage amyloid clumps that eventually form plaques. By clearing these early aggregates, lecanemab prevents new plaques from forming and slows disease progression at an earlier stage. In contrast, donanemab binds to fully formed plaques, making it more aggressive in plaque removal (Alzheimer's Association, 2024b).

Another key difference is the dosing frequency and treatment duration. Lecanemab is initially given every two weeks and has recently been approved for a once-monthly maintenance dose after 18 months. In contrast, donanemab is given every four weeks from the start and may be discontinued once amyloid plaques are sufficiently cleared. This means that donanemab has the potential for a shorter treatment duration, depending on how quickly a patient responds.

Both drugs have been shown to slow cognitive decline, but their effectiveness varies. In clinical trials, lecanemab slowed cognitive decline by 27% over 18 months, while donanemab reduced decline by 29%, with greater benefits observed in patients who began treatment early, before significant tau buildup (another harmful protein associated with Alzheimer's) (Epsay et al., 2024). However, donanemab also carries a higher risk of amyloid-related imaging abnormalities (ARIA), which can cause brain swelling or microbleeds, requiring close monitoring.

Choosing between donanemab and lecanemab depends on several factors, including a patient's stage of disease, overall health, and tolerance for potential side effects. Donanemab may be preferable for patients seeking a more aggressive amyloid-clearing approach with the possibility of stopping treatment, while lecanemab offers a strategy focused on long-term plaque prevention and gradual disease slowing. Both treatments represent significant advancements in Alzheimer's care, providing new options for patients and their families.

FDA-Approved Medications to Manage Symptoms

Additionally, there are several drugs that address cognitive symptoms but do not halt disease progression.

Brexpiprazole

Brexpiprazole is an atypical antipsychotic used to manage agitation in people with Alzheimer's disease. Agitation can include symptoms such as restlessness, aggression, irritability, pacing, yelling, or resistance to care. These behaviors can be distressing for both patients and caregivers. Brexpiprazole works by altering the activity of dopamine and serotonin, two brain chemicals involved in mood, behavior, and perception. It partially stimulates dopamine and serotonin receptors while blocking certain serotonin signals, helping to stabilize mood and reduce agitation. While it can be effective, potential side effects include dizziness, cold-like symptoms, high blood sugar, and an increased risk of stroke, especially in older adults with dementia-related psychosis (National Institute on Aging, 2023c).

Donepezil

Donepezil is a cholinesterase inhibitor that helps with cognitive symptoms of Alzheimer's, such as memory loss, confusion, and difficulty with thinking and reasoning. It works by increasing acetylcholine, a chemical that nerve cells use to communicate. In Alzheimer's, acetylcholine levels drop, leading to problems with learning and memory. Donepezil slows this decline by preventing acetylcholine from breaking down too quickly, allowing brain cells to communicate more effectively. This can lead to modest improvements in memory, attention, and the ability to perform daily activities. Common side effects include nausea, vomiting, diarrhea, trouble sleeping, muscle cramps, fatigue, and weight loss (National Institute on Aging, 2023c).

Galantamine

Galantamine is another cholinesterase inhibitor used for mild to moderate Alzheimer's, targeting cognitive symptoms such as memory impairment and confusion. Like donepezil, it prevents the breakdown of acetylcholine, but it also stimulates nicotinic receptors, which help release more acetylcholine in the brain. This dual action may enhance its effectiveness in improving memory and cognitive function. However, galantamine does not stop disease progression. Instead, it temporarily slows symptom worsening. Possible side effects include nausea, vomiting, diarrhea, decreased appetite, weight loss, dizziness, and headaches (National Institute on Aging, 2023c).

Benzgalantamine

Benzgalantamine is a modified form of galantamine developed to reduce some of its common side effects, particularly digestive issues like nausea and vomiting. It still works by increasing acetylcholine levels and stimulating nicotinic receptors to enhance memory and cognitive function in mild to moderate

Alzheimer's. Since it is a variation of galantamine, it provides similar benefits but may be better tolerated by some patients (National Institute on Aging, 2023c).

Memantine

Memantine is an NMDA receptor antagonist used for moderate to severe Alzheimer's. It primarily addresses cognitive symptoms such as confusion, difficulty with problem-solving, and struggles with daily tasks by regulating glutamate activity in the brain. Glutamate is important for learning and memory, but in Alzheimer's, excessive amounts can overstimulate nerve cells, leading to damage. Memantine blocks excessive glutamate while still allowing normal brain signaling. This may help people with advanced Alzheimer's maintain their ability to perform everyday activities for a longer period. Side effects may include dizziness, headache, diarrhea, constipation, and confusion (National Institute on Aging, 2023c).

A combination of memantine and donepezil is prescribed for moderate to severe Alzheimer's to manage cognitive decline more effectively. Memantine protects neurons from the damaging effects of excess glutamate, while donepezil boosts acetylcholine levels to improve memory and thinking. This combination may help patients maintain their ability to communicate, recognize loved ones, and carry out daily tasks for longer than either drug alone. Common side effects include headache, nausea, vomiting, diarrhea, dizziness, loss of appetite, and small bruises (National Institute on Aging, 2023c).

Rivastigmine

Rivastigmine is another cholinesterase inhibitor that treats mild to severe Alzheimer's, targeting memory loss, confusion, and difficulties with reasoning. Unlike donepezil and galantamine, rivastigmine prevents the breakdown of both acetylcholine and butyrylcholine, another brain chemical involved in cognitive function. By preserving these neurotransmitters, rivastigmine may help slow the decline in thinking and memory skills. It is available in capsule, liquid, and transdermal patch forms. Possible side effects include nausea, vomiting, diarrhea, weight loss, indigestion, decreased appetite, anorexia, and muscle weakness (National Institute on Aging, 2023c).

Emerging Treatments

New treatments are also in development, targeting various brain changes associated with Alzheimer's, including tau buildup and inflammation. Currently, 156 clinical trials are underway to explore additional therapies (Alzheimer's Association 2024).

Therapeutic Plasma Exchange

Therapeutic Plasma Exchange (TPE) is a medical procedure that involves the selective removal of plasma from a patient's blood to extract pathological substances, such as abnormal proteins, immune complexes, autoantibodies, and toxins. The treatment is designed to remove molecules contributing to disease while simultaneously replacing the removed plasma with a substitute, typically albumin, or other beneficial plasma components. This process is used to treat a variety of neurological, immunological, and hematological disorders, where abnormal substances in the plasma are implicated in disease progression (Rohrer et al., 2022).

One potential mechanism for the efficacy of TPE in Alzheimer's treatment lies in its ability to manipulate the concentration gradient of amyloid peptides. TPE works by removing peptides from the bloodstream, reducing their circulating levels, and potentially preventing further deposition in the brain. By lowering peripheral amyloid-beta concentrations, TPE may influence the balance between the deposition and clearance of these peptides within the central nervous system (Rohrer et al., 2022).

In addition to amyloid-beta peptide removal, TPE also infuses albumin into the patient's system. Albumin, a protein commonly found in blood plasma, has multiple functions, including the binding and transport of molecules. Some studies suggest that albumin could play a protective role by binding to toxic molecules, such as amyloid-beta peptides, thereby preventing their neurotoxic effects. Albumin may also support the maintenance of vascular health and reduce blood-brain barrier dysfunction, which is often seen in Alzheimer's disease. These combined effects of amyloid-beta clearance and albumin infusion form the theoretical basis for TPE's potential benefit in Alzheimer's treatment (Rohrer et al., 2022).

While the rationale behind using TPE to treat Alzheimer's appears promising, the clinical evidence supporting its effectiveness remains limited. Several studies have been conducted to explore the efficacy of TPE in Alzheimer's patients, although the results have been mixed. Some early-phase clinical trials have demonstrated improvements in cognitive function and reductions in amyloid levels following TPE treatment. However, these findings are not consistent across all studies, and larger, more rigorously designed trials are necessary to draw definitive conclusions (Rohrer et al., 2022).

Chapter 6

Holistic Approaches to Dementia Care

In this chapter, we will cover various holistic treatments for Alzheimer's disease that complement traditional medical approaches. These treatments aim to address the emotional, cognitive, and physical well-being of patients, offering a more comprehensive approach to managing the disease. This chapter will explore the mechanisms, benefits, and limitations of several therapies, highlighting their potential to improve the quality of life for individuals with Alzheimer's.

Cognitive Stimulation Therapy (CST)

Cognitive Stimulation Therapy (CST) is an evidence-based intervention designed to improve cognitive function and overall quality of life for individuals with mild to moderate dementia.

CST typically occurs in group sessions led by trained facilitators, who guide participants through a series of activities that stimulate memory, concentration, and mental engagement. The goal of CST is to promote neuroplasticity by encouraging individuals to actively participate in cognitive exercises that engage various mental faculties. These activities often include discussions, problem-solving tasks, puzzles, and creative exercises, all of which provide mental stimulation that can strengthen existing neural connections or form new ones (Mackrani, 2023b).

A growing body of research supports the effectiveness of CST. Numerous studies have demonstrated significant benefits, particularly in terms of cognitive function and quality of life. For instance, a study conducted in 2014 found that participants who engaged in CST experienced considerable improvements in their quality of life, with effects lasting up to six months after completing the program. In addition, a 2019 review of multiple studies confirmed that CST had moderate positive effects on cognitive functions such as language comprehension and attention (Mackrani, 2023b). These results suggest that CST can provide lasting cognitive and emotional benefits, making it a valuable tool in dementia care.

CST sessions often involve a variety of activities, such as reminiscence sessions, word association games, and creative arts. These activities encourage participants to reflect on their memories, engage with others, and use their cognitive skills in a supportive and social environment. The variety of tasks involved in CST helps keep the sessions interesting and engaging, which in turn boosts the likelihood of sustained participation and continued benefits.

Music Therapy

Music therapy has garnered significant attention for its ability to stimulate neuroplasticity in individuals with dementia. It encompasses both active methods, such as singing or playing musical instruments, and receptive methods, like listening to music. The therapeutic potential of music lies in its ability to engage different brain regions, particularly those associated with memory, emotion, and motor control. Research suggests that music has a unique capacity to evoke emotional responses and memories, often triggering reactions in individuals with dementia who may have difficulty communicating through words (Mackrani, 2023a).

Music remains a powerful stimulus even as other cognitive abilities decline in individuals with dementia. This is because the brain's ability to process music and respond emotionally to it often remains intact for longer than other forms of cognitive processing. Music therapy can enhance communication, provide emotional comfort, and improve social interactions by encouraging non-verbal expression and connection. Additionally, music therapy can help reduce agitation, anxiety, and depression, which are common symptoms in individuals with dementia.

By stimulating brain areas involved in memory and emotion, music therapy offers a unique and effective way to maintain cognitive function and emotional well-being. In particular, it can support the brain's neuroplasticity by encouraging the formation of new connections between neural circuits and by reinforcing existing ones. As a non-invasive, enjoyable, and cost-effective approach, music therapy is increasingly being integrated into dementia care programs worldwide.

Art Therapy

Art therapy, which involves individuals expressing themselves through various forms of visual art, has shown positive impacts on emotional health and cognitive function in individuals with dementia. This form of therapy provides a creative outlet for self-expression, allowing individuals to communicate emotions and thoughts in a non-verbal way. Art therapy has been linked to improvements in both communication skills and mental health, particularly in reducing symptoms of anxiety and depression.

Longitudinal studies on art therapy have demonstrated that engaging in creative activities can help individuals with dementia maintain or improve their cognitive abilities, including memory recall and problem-solving skills. Beyond cognitive improvements, art therapy also offers emotional benefits by providing participants with a sense of accomplishment and self-worth. The process of creating art allows individuals to engage with their emotions in a meaningful and constructive manner, which can enhance mood and reduce feelings of isolation (Mackrani, 2023a).

Furthermore, art therapy can stimulate the brain's plasticity by engaging multiple cognitive pathways, including those associated with creativity, perception, and motor skills. This process may help strengthen neural connections and provide a positive experience that cultivates emotional resilience in the face of cognitive decline. As a complementary treatment, art therapy plays an important role in holistic care, offering a multifaceted approach to supporting individuals with dementia.

Reminiscence Therapy

Reminiscence therapy, which often includes life story work, involves discussing past events and experiences with individuals living with dementia. This approach uses sensory cues, such as photographs, objects, and sounds, to evoke memories and facilitate storytelling. Reminiscence therapy aims to stimulate brain areas associated with long-term memory and emotion, helping individuals reconnect with their personal history and engage in meaningful conversations.

Studies have shown that reminiscence therapy can reduce symptoms of anxiety and depression in individuals with dementia while also supporting their sense of identity (ARIIA, 2024). By encouraging the recall of positive memories and providing an opportunity for social interaction, reminiscence therapy helps individuals feel more connected to themselves and others. It also improves communication skills by reinforcing the use of language and facilitating emotional expression.

In addition to the benefits for individuals with dementia, reminiscence therapy also has a positive impact on caregivers and family members. By learning about the individual's life experiences and personal history, caregivers can gain a deeper understanding of their needs and preferences, which can improve care and strengthen relationships (ARIIA, 2024). This aspect of reminiscence therapy highlights the importance of maintaining identity and personal continuity throughout the progression of dementia.

Transcranial Magnetic Stimulation (TMS)

Transcranial Magnetic Stimulation (TMS) is a non-invasive technique that uses magnetic fields to stimulate specific regions of the brain. A coil placed on the scalp generates pulses of magnetic energy, which induce electrical currents that alter neural activity. TMS has been primarily used to treat conditions like depression, anxiety, and chronic pain, but its potential benefits for neuroplasticity have also garnered significant attention.

By targeting specific brain areas, TMS can encourage the brain to reorganize itself and form new neural connections in response to stimulation. This process is particularly valuable in the context of dementia, as it may help restore cognitive function and slow the progression of the disease. Research has demonstrated that TMS can enhance synaptic connectivity and increase the release of neurotransmitters, leading to improvements in learning, memory, and motor skills (Weiler et al., 2020).

TMS has shown promise in aiding rehabilitation after brain injuries or strokes, as well as in enhancing cognitive function in individuals with neurodegenerative diseases. Its ability to facilitate neuroplasticity makes it a promising tool for dementia care, potentially offering a new avenue for treating cognitive decline and improving brain health.

Acupuncture and Acupressure

Acupuncture and acupressure are non-pharmacologic therapies that can be used to address the behavioral and psychological symptoms of dementia. These symptoms, often referred to as BPSD, are prevalent in individuals diagnosed with dementia, especially during the middle stages of the disease. The symptoms can vary widely and may include depression, anxiety, aggression, irritability, and agitation. BPSD significantly affects the quality of life of individuals with dementia and their caregivers, and it often leads to increased stress, caregiver burden, and healthcare costs. In some cases, these symptoms may also result in early institutionalization or placement in long-term care settings (Harris, 2019).

Traditional treatment approaches for BPSD often involve the use of medications such as antipsychotics, anti-anxiety medications, and antidepressants. However, these medications have shown limited efficacy in managing these symptoms and can have serious side effects, particularly in older adults. For example, antipsychotics have been associated with increased mortality rates in elderly individuals with dementia, while anti-anxiety medications such as benzodiazepines can worsen cognitive function and increase the risk of falls. As a result, there has been growing interest in non-pharmacologic interventions as an alternative means of managing BPSD.

Acupuncture, based on the principles of Traditional Chinese Medicine, involves the stimulation of specific points on the body known as acupoints. This stimulation is believed to restore the balance of energy, or "qi," within the body, thereby addressing various health issues. Acupuncture typically uses fine needles that are inserted into the skin at specific acupoints, although other methods, such as electrical stimulation, may also be used. Acupressure, on the other hand, involves the application of manual pressure to these acupoints without the use of needles. Both acupuncture and acupressure aim to regulate the flow of energy within the body and are believed to help treat a wide range of symptoms, including pain, anxiety, depression, and cognitive dysfunction (Harris, 2019).

Research has shown that acupuncture and acupressure may have beneficial effects on individuals with dementia. For instance, studies have demonstrated that acupuncture can help improve cognitive function and alleviate symptoms of depression and anxiety in people with dementia. Brain imaging studies have also shown that acupuncture can activate areas of the brain responsible for cognitive function. These findings suggest that acupuncture and acupressure may help stimulate the central nervous system and influence the release of neurotransmitters and hormones that are involved in mood regulation and cognitive processing (Harris, 2019).

In addition to their potential effects on cognitive function and mood, acupuncture and acupressure may also help manage other BPSD symptoms, such as agitation and aggression. The relaxation effects of acupuncture and acupressure may help reduce the frequency and intensity of these behaviors, thereby improving the quality of life for both individuals with dementia and their caregivers.

While much of the research on acupuncture and acupressure for dementia has been conducted in countries where Traditional Chinese Medicine is widely practiced, there is a growing interest in these therapies in Western healthcare settings. More studies are needed to determine the efficacy of acupuncture and acupressure in Western populations, as well as to establish guidelines for their use in dementia care.

Overall, acupuncture and acupressure offer promising non-pharmacologic treatments for managing the behavioral and psychological symptoms of dementia. These therapies provide a safe and effective alternative to medications, with minimal side effects, and can improve the overall well-being of individuals with dementia and their caregivers. Further research is required to expand the understanding and application of these therapies in Western healthcare systems (Harris, 2019).

Mindfulness-Based Interventions

Mindfulness-based interventions (MBIs) are another promising non-drug treatment option for individuals with Alzheimer's disease, especially in its early stages. These interventions focus on increasing awareness and promoting emotional regulation through practices like meditation and mindful attention. The findings from a preliminary pilot study by Giulietti et al. (2023) support the idea that MBIs can significantly improve the quality of life, mood, and cognitive abilities of older adults with Alzheimer's disease, potentially slowing the progression of the condition.

The study outlined that mindfulness can manage Alzheimer's in the following ways:

- **Improved Quality of Life and Mood**: The study showed that after six months of mindfulness training, participants experienced notable improvements in several aspects of their quality of life. These improvements included better physical functioning, fewer emotional problems, reduced fatigue, better social interactions, and a decrease in pain. Mood also significantly improved, as patients felt more emotionally balanced and less distressed by the symptoms of Alzheimer's. In contrast, patients who did not receive mindfulness training showed worsening conditions in all these areas over the same period.
- **Cognitive Benefits**: One of the main concerns in Alzheimer's disease is cognitive decline. However, the study found that mindfulness practice helped prevent further degeneration in cognitive abilities. For example, patients in the mindfulness group did not experience the usual decline in cognitive functions such as attention, memory, and visuospatial skills, while those in the untreated group showed worsening in these areas. The study suggests that mindfulness may help stabilize

cognitive abilities and could even slow the rate of cognitive decline.

- **Reduction of Neuropsychiatric Symptoms**: Neuropsychiatric symptoms, such as depression, anxiety, apathy, and aggression, are common in Alzheimer's patients and can significantly affect their quality of life. The results from the mindfulness group showed a reduction in several of these symptoms, including decreased agitation, anxiety, and irritability, as well as improvements in sleep and appetite. In contrast, the untreated group experienced an increase in these symptoms, especially apathy, which is a common and troubling aspect of Alzheimer's disease. The reduction in depression and apathy, in particular, suggests that mindfulness may help address the emotional aspects of Alzheimer's, improving patients' overall mood and engagement with their surroundings.

- **Emotional Regulation**: Mindfulness is known to help individuals regulate their emotions, and this effect is especially important for people with Alzheimer's disease. The practice encourages focusing on the present moment with a non-judgmental attitude, which can reduce mental distractions and help patients maintain focus on their current experiences. This improved emotional regulation can decrease stress and anxiety, both of which are known to exacerbate cognitive decline in aging individuals. By reducing these negative emotional states, mindfulness helps protect against the worsening of cognitive and emotional symptoms associated with Alzheimer's.

- **Socialization and Support in Group Settings**: Another key benefit of MBIs is the group setting in which they are often conducted. Alzheimer's patients, particularly those in the early stages, may still have moments of lucidity and awareness about their cognitive decline. This awareness can lead to isolation and emotional distress. Participating in a group mindfulness practice helps create a supportive environment where patients can share their experiences with others who understand their struggles. This sense of community can reduce feelings of loneliness and help patients manage the emotional stress that often accompanies Alzheimer's. Additionally, social support is essential for maintaining emotional well-being, and group mindfulness settings offer both a therapeutic space for emotional expression and a means to foster solidarity among participants (Giulietti, 2023).

The effectiveness of mindfulness practices in Alzheimer's patients likely stems from their ability to address both cognitive and emotional challenges. Mindfulness training helps patients focus their attention and regulate their emotions, reducing the mental distractions that contribute to cognitive decline. It also helps manage emotional states like anxiety and depression, which are known to worsen the symptoms of Alzheimer's disease. The ability to manage these emotional states may reduce the negative impact they have on cognitive performance, slowing down the overall progression of the disease.

One possible explanation for the observed improvements in cognitive performance is that mindfulness training increases the ability to maintain alertness and focus. This heightened attention and reduced emotional disturbance can lead to better performance in everyday cognitive tasks, such as remembering names, maintaining concentration, and navigating familiar environments. This improved cognitive ability might help patients maintain their independence for a longer period.

A key finding of the study was that patients who participated in mindfulness training for six months experienced more significant improvements than those who received shorter interventions, which is common in many mindfulness studies. This suggests that for Alzheimer's patients, a longer duration of mindfulness practice may be necessary to achieve meaningful benefits. Given that Alzheimer's disease involves complex, long-term cognitive and emotional degeneration, shorter mindfulness interventions may not provide enough time for significant changes in patients' overall well-being and cognitive health.

Given the findings, it is reasonable to propose that mindfulness-based interventions could serve as a secondary prevention strategy for Alzheimer's disease. By introducing mindfulness practices early in the disease process, it may be possible to slow the progression of cognitive decline and improve patients' overall quality of life. Additionally, mindfulness could reduce the emotional distress associated with the disease, helping patients maintain better relationships and feel more connected to their environment.

One of the simplest ways to integrate mindfulness into daily life is through breathing exercises. These exercises help center the mind, offering a pause button for the racing thoughts that often accompany stress and anxiety. A few minutes of deep, focused breathing can relax the body and mind, creating a sense of calm and focus. Imagine sitting comfortably, closing your eyes, and taking a slow, deep breath in through your nose, holding it for a moment, and then exhaling slowly through your mouth. This simple exercise can be done anywhere and anytime, providing an immediate sense of relief and grounding.

While the results of this study are promising, it is important to note that the research had some limitations. The sample size was small, and the participants came from a single institution, which may not be representative of all Alzheimer's patients. Further studies with larger and more diverse populations would help confirm these findings and expand our understanding of how mindfulness can be applied to different stages of Alzheimer's disease.

Moreover, the effectiveness of mindfulness training at various stages of Alzheimer's disease and whether it remains effective in more advanced stages requires further exploration. Future studies should also investigate the long-term effects of mindfulness practices and whether continued training or periodic reinforcement of mindfulness techniques is necessary to maintain benefits over time (Giulietti, 2023).

In this chapter, we covered a range of holistic treatments that offer supportive care for Alzheimer's patients. From the cognitive stimulation provided by music, art, and reminiscence therapy to the brain-stimulating effects of TMS and mindfulness, each method presents unique benefits. While research is ongoing, the integration of these therapies alongside conventional treatments holds promise for enhancing patient outcomes, improving emotional well-being, and maintaining cognitive function. As these practices continue to evolve, they may play an increasingly important role in managing Alzheimer's disease holistically.

However, despite their promising effects, these therapies are not without limitations. Standardizing non-pharmacological interventions can be challenging, as their effectiveness may vary from person to person. Nevertheless, the positive outcomes experienced by many patients highlight the importance of incorporating these therapies into comprehensive dementia care plans. In our next chapter, we will look at the latest technological advancements and how they are improving dementia care.

Chapter 7

Technological Innovations in Dementia Care

In this chapter, we will explore the role of technological innovation in dementia care, focusing on its potential to improve quality of life and reduce caregiver burden. Advancements in digital tools have opened new possibilities for supporting individuals with dementia and their caregivers. From cognitive offloading and automated task management to remote monitoring and symptom treatment, technology offers a range of solutions tailored to different stages of the disease. Additionally, innovations in emotional and social support can help combat the isolation often experienced by those with dementia. We will discuss the various types of technology currently in use, examine their benefits and limitations, and consider the future implications of these tools in enhancing dementia care.

In 2007, Dishman and Carrillo highlighted how the growing availability of "everyday technologies" could revolutionize the care of individuals with Alzheimer's disease and related dementias (ADRD). This led to the launch of the Everyday Technologies for Alzheimer's Care initiative, aimed at promoting research in this area. A 2009 progress report from the initiative revealed that home computers, cell phones, and broadband internet were increasingly used by middle-aged and older adults. These technologies showed potential to improve diagnostic accuracy, track disease progression, enhance symptom treatment, and reduce caregiver burden (Kiselica et al., 2024).

Supporting caregivers is especially important, given their central role in the lives of those with ADRD. Family and friends provide care in 90% of dementia cases, contributing an estimated $339.5 billion annually (Kiselica et al., 2024). These unpaid caregivers assist with daily activities and coordinate care across various settings. While caregivers find value in their role, they also experience more financial stress, poorer physical health, disrupted sleep, and higher rates of mental illness compared to those not involved in caregiving.

After more than a decade of investment and research, technological supports for caregivers have significantly increased. Moreover, a new area of scholarship has emerged focused on digital biomarkers, which could enable rapid, widespread diagnosis and symptom monitoring. Technologies have also been applied to deliver existing interventions, such as adapting multimodal risk reduction programs for the internet, and to develop new treatment approaches, such as technology-based training to improve daily functioning.

Pathways to Improve Caregiving

Caregiving is complex, with the specific needs of care varying depending on the underlying illness, disease stage, care environment, and other factors. Developing a comprehensive framework for technology in caregiving requires identifying common pathways through which existing digital technologies can influence care, as well as the outcomes that technology-based interventions should aim to achieve. Below, we examine five core pathways by which technology can improve caregiving, along with potential outcome measures to assess its impact.

Cognitive Offloading

Cognitive offloading refers to transferring a mental task to a digital or physical memory aid. For individuals with mild to moderate ADRD, smartphone personal assistant apps can help achieve this by storing to-do lists and sending automated reminders to assist with task completion.

An example of this in caregiving is using Apple's Siri to issue a voice command like, "Remind me to give Dad his medications at 9:00 PM," with the device then sending a push notification at the specified time. This technology reduces the reliance on caregivers' own memory, addressing the common caregiving burden of managing not only their own daily tasks but also those of the person with ADRD.

Outcome measures for cognitive offloading could include behavioral markers such as medication adherence rates and the reduction of subjective caregiver cognitive burden (the "mental load" of caregiving). This aspect is under-researched; current scales measuring caregiving burden do not adequately capture cognitive load, presenting an opportunity to create new metrics (Kiselica et al., 2024).

Automated Task Management

Automated task management focuses on simplifying caregiving tasks to reduce the time caregivers spend on routine activities. Many caregivers of individuals with ADRD spend significant time on activities like grocery shopping and managing finances. Digital tools such as grocery delivery apps (e.g., Instacart) and autopay for bills can streamline these tasks, saving time and reducing caregiver stress.

Outcome measures for this pathway could include the time spent on caregiving tasks and caregiver burden, as measured by scales such as the Impact of Dementia on Caregivers (IDC). Usability of the technology must also be considered to ensure that these tools are accessible and reliable, as complicated or ineffective technologies could worsen caregiver burden. Therefore, including measures such as the System Usability Scale is important (Kiselica et al., 2024).

Remote Monitoring and Intervention

Remote monitoring and intervention can address safety concerns and reduce caregiver strain by allowing care partners to monitor individuals with ADRD remotely. Technologies like bed sensors and depth cameras paired with safety alerts can help reduce wandering, falls, and other risky behaviors. Such technologies provide caregivers with peace of mind, allowing them to leave the home or engage in other activities without constant worry.

Outcome measures for remote monitoring could focus on both objective safety events (e.g., falls, wandering) and more subjective caregiver outcomes, such as loneliness or perceptions of isolation. Existing tools like the UCLA Loneliness Scale and the Burden

Scale for Family Caregivers can help assess these impacts (Kiselica et al., 2024).

Emotional and Social Support

This section addresses the emotional strain that caregiving often involves. Many care partners report high levels of distress and lack of information about dementia services. Accessing online resources, such as caregiver support groups or educational websites (e.g., Alzheimer's Association), can provide valuable assistance. Additionally, apps like Brain CareNotes offer psychoeducational resources and expert guidance to help caregivers manage caregiving challenges.

Outcome measures for this pathway could include caregiver mood (e.g., using the Patient Health Questionnaire-9) and caregiving knowledge (e.g., Dementia Care Knowledge Assessment). It would also be important to examine whether these resources improve the quality of life for individuals with ADRD using scales like the Quality of Life in Alzheimer's Disease scale (Kiselica et al., 2024).

Symptom Treatment

Finally, symptom treatment through technology is aimed at reducing neurobehavioral symptoms common in ADRD, such as aggression or apathy. One example is the use of PARO, an animatronic social robot designed to simulate animal interactions. PARO is a therapeutic robot designed specifically to assist individuals with dementia, offering emotional support and engagement. Developed by AIST (National Institute of Advanced Industrial Science and Technology) in Japan, PARO resembles a baby seal and is equipped with advanced sensors, allowing it to respond to touch, sound, and light. This robot has been designed to provide comfort and companionship, mimicking the behaviors of a real pet, which has been shown to have therapeutic effects on patients with dementia, especially those suffering from social isolation.

PARO is programmed to interact with its user, responding to petting, speech, and other stimuli with various movements, such as tilting its head, opening its eyes, and making sounds. These interactions help stimulate emotional responses, promoting feelings of relaxation and improving the overall well-being of the individual. Research has shown that the use of PARO can reduce anxiety and agitation, which are common symptoms in dementia patients. The robot also encourages social interaction, as patients often initiate conversation or connect with caregivers through their engagement with PARO (Sense Medical Limited, 2024).

Adapting Technology Use According to Disease Stage

Dementia progresses through distinct stages, and the use of technology to improve outcomes for individuals with ADRD, as well as their care partners, will vary depending on the stage of the disease. The potential benefits and challenges of technology use also shift with disease progression.

Initially, in the asymptomatic preclinical phase (Stage 1), individuals with ADRD will test positive for Alzheimer's disease biomarkers but show no noticeable clinical changes. At this stage, care partners may still be in the role of "pre-care partners," as the individual requires minimal assistance. The person with preclinical Alzheimer's disease retains sufficient independence to engage with technology, often with support from the care partner. Interventions during this phase could focus on recognizing early warning signs and preparing for future needs. Technology could also be used to promote cognitive reserve and reduce the risk of future decline. Additionally, the preclinical phase presents a prime opportunity for learning new technology skills and establishing habits, which may become more challenging to maintain in later stages due to cognitive and functional decline.

Technologies could also assist in symptom tracking, helping detect early cognitive changes. For instance, researchers have explored using data collected from commonly used devices like smartphones or computers. By applying artificial intelligence algorithms to this data, subtle shifts in activity patterns, social interactions, and language use could be identified, flagging potential cognitive decline.

As the disease progresses into transitional cognitive decline (Stage 2) and mild cognitive impairment (Stage 3), care partners increasingly help patients incorporate technology for compensatory strategies. Technology may shift toward offloading cognitive tasks and automating daily activities to reduce errors and maintain task efficiency. However, a potential issue at this stage is an overreliance on technology, which could detract from simpler, more effective non-digital strategies. For instance, a written reminder placed above the stove might prove just as effective as a digital alert.

When functional decline becomes more evident in Stage 4 (mild dementia), the patient may depend more heavily on technology to manage daily tasks independently. Care partners are also likely to rely on technology to manage their increasing responsibilities. A downside of this dependency is that care partners could feel overwhelmed by trying to coordinate multiple devices and applications, inadvertently increasing their caregiving burden.

In the moderate and severe dementia phases (Stages 5 and 6), the patient's ability to engage with technology will diminish, and they will be at a higher risk for health and safety concerns, such as wandering or falls. At this point, care partners will likely take over most technology-based tasks, focusing primarily on symptom management and safety monitoring. However, technology use in these stages raises concerns about privacy and autonomy, as patients may feel that surveillance tools infringe upon their independence. One study found that while care partners favored using surveillance technology to track wandering behavior, individuals with dementia felt that these measures compromised their autonomy and were stigmatizing (Kiselica et al., 2024).

Limitations of Technology

Despite the promising potential of technologies in ADRD care, there is a digital divide that limits access to these solutions among certain groups. Digital disadvantage refers to the unequal ownership and use of technology due to factors such as socioeconomic status, education, and institutional barriers. For instance, a 2023 Pew Research survey revealed that broadband access is significantly lower among Black (68%) and Hispanic (75%) populations compared to White (83%) and Asian (84%) individuals (Kiselica et al., 2024).

Moreover, research shows that the intersection of race, ethnicity, and socioeconomic status further exacerbates disparities in technology access and usage. People in disadvantaged groups, especially non-white and lower-income individuals, are less likely to use the internet to obtain health information. Researchers hypothesize that individuals facing the greatest digital disadvantage stand to benefit most from technology-based interventions in ADRD care (Kiselica et al., 2024). However, it is also possible that the barriers these groups face may hinder their ability to fully benefit from technological solutions. Future research should examine whether outcomes of technology interventions differ depending on the digital disadvantage of the patient and care partner.

In conclusion, technological innovations in dementia care have the potential to transform the way individuals with dementia and their caregivers manage the challenges of the condition. While these tools offer significant benefits in areas such as cognitive support, task management, and emotional well-being, they also present challenges that require careful consideration. In the next chapter, we will look at some of the important ethical considerations of dementia care.

Chapter 8

Ethical Considerations in Dementia Care

In this chapter, we will discuss the ethical considerations involved in dementia care, focusing on the challenges that arise at different stages of the disease. We will examine the complexities of communicating a diagnosis, including the ethical dilemmas surrounding truth-telling and disclosure. The use of genetic and biomarker testing raises concerns about informed consent, psychological impact, and potential discrimination. Decision-making capacity assessments become increasingly important as dementia progresses, requiring thoughtful approaches to advance care planning and surrogate decision-making. Symptom and behavioral management present ethical challenges, particularly in balancing patient dignity with safety.

We will also explore the broader societal implications of dementia care, including financial burdens, caregiver responsibilities, and disparities in healthcare access. Finally, we will consider the ethical concerns associated with artificial intelligence in dementia care, including issues of privacy, surveillance, and deception.

Ultimately, a comprehensive understanding of these ethical issues helps healthcare providers, caregivers, and policymakers make informed, compassionate decisions that improve the quality of life for individuals with dementia and their families.

Complexities in Communicating the Diagnosis

In communicating the diagnosis, clinicians may find that patients and family members often have different understandings of terms such as "dementia" and "Alzheimer's disease." Because the term dementia has lay connotations of insanity and mental deficiency, some experts have argued for abolishing the term as hurtful and derogatory. The most recent edition of the DSM-5 generally omits references to dementia in favor of a more general term, "major neurocognitive disorder." Although we retain the term dementia, it should be used with sensitivity and awareness of potential negative connotations. Furthermore, when communicating with patients and families, neurologists should acknowledge widespread misconceptions and clarify what they mean by the term dementia, also acknowledging that its use by other clinicians may be different (Chiong et al, 2021).

Not All Dementia Is the Same

While Alzheimer's is the most common form of dementia, patients and families may benefit from knowing that Alzheimer's is only one among many different causes of dementia, that dementia is not exclusively a disease of advanced age, and that symptoms can differ significantly across individual patients. For instance, although dementia may be commonly understood to primarily involve memory impairment, mood and behavioral changes often have more of an effect on patients and families than declines in memory or cognitive function. Thus, expectations based on observing other patients or on cognitive test scores may not predict the most consequential features of the patient's clinical course.

Because dementia is often considered to be exclusively a disease of aging, middle-aged and younger patients with conditions such as early-onset Alzheimer's, frontotemporal dementia, and Huntington disease face unique problems, as do their families. As earlier onset forms of dementia often present with socioemotional and behavioral disturbances before typical cognitive complaints, diagnosis of sporadic disease is often delayed, and patients' behaviors may be misinterpreted as manifestations of a psychiatric rather than a neurologic disorder. Such patients are often mid-career rather than retired and may have children at home, increasing safety concerns and burdens for other family members. Community resources such as adult day programs, nursing facilities, and caregiver support groups are also often designed principally for the needs of older patients. Clinicians should anticipate devoting greater time to caregiver education and identifying resources for such patients; referral to specialty centers is often also useful (Chiong et al, 2021).

Truth-Telling and Disclosure

Another ethical consideration for health professionals is disclosure. Prior to communicating a diagnosis, it is important to ascertain how much information patients wish to receive and how they prefer to receive information. Some patients defer to family members or other trusted people who can receive information on their behalf. In the past, clinicians have sometimes invoked therapeutic privilege to justify withholding information (such as a diagnosis of dementia) deemed too devastating or otherwise harmful to the patient, and clinicians now may receive requests from family members to withhold a diagnosis from the patient due to related concerns. However, unless patients who have capacity specifically make a request that such information be given to others rather than directly to them, such nondisclosure violates patient autonomy, undermines trust, reinforces stigma, and may deprive patients and families of important opportunities to plan for future needs. For patients without decisional capacity, the diagnosis should be disclosed to a legally recognized surrogate decision-maker and, in most cases, also to the patient. In some cases, disclosure to the patient may require planning with the surrogate.

It is important to consider the setting and manner of disclosure to minimize the risk of emotional harm to the patient. For instance, involving another clinician with a longstanding relationship with the patient, or facilitating the presence of family members or other loved ones, can provide support and assist in recalling details that patients with memory disorders are prone to forget. Involvement of trusted family and friends can also prevent misunderstanding of patients' symptoms and behavior, mitigate social isolation, and facilitate advance care planning. In most cases, family members' fears about potential emotional harm can be assuaged by thoughtful and compassionate disclosure using these strategies (Chiong et al, 2021).

Genetic and Biomarker Testing in Dementia Ethics

Degenerative dementias are primarily influenced by a combination of genetic, environmental, and lifestyle factors, although they may rarely result from monogenic mutations. A growing array of tests is now available, which can be used to confirm the cause of dementia in symptomatic individuals or suggest future cognitive decline in asymptomatic or presymptomatic individuals. Ethical considerations surrounding these tests depend on factors such as the context (clinical or research), whether the patient is symptomatic or at risk for dementia, the potential impact on family members, and whether the test is intended for diagnosis or to indicate increased risk.

Diagnostic Use of Genetic Testing

Genetic testing is often diagnostic in symptomatic patients with dominantly inherited dementias, such as Huntington's disease, familial Alzheimer's, frontotemporal dementia, and prion diseases. It can also predict the onset of these conditions in presymptomatic carriers of pathogenic genetic variants. However, other genetic markers, such as the APOE gene, are not diagnostic but instead modify an individual's risk of developing dementia. Furthermore, cerebrospinal fluid and PET biomarkers detecting amyloid and tau aggregation are now being used to diagnose patients with atypical forms of dementia. In research settings, these biomarkers can even identify pathologic changes in asymptomatic individuals, which raises ethical questions about using them to predict clinical Alzheimer's in healthy people (Chiong et al, 2021).

Ethical Concerns in Genetic and Biomarker Testing

Clinical research is advancing rapidly in the realm of genetic and biomarker testing, significantly enhancing our understanding of Alzheimer's and other dementias. However, the translation of these tools into clinical practice presents ethical challenges. Early and accurate diagnosis can be beneficial, offering opportunities for diagnostic closure, family planning, and advance care planning. On the other hand, testing asymptomatic individuals can result in potential harm, including adverse psychological effects, confusion from genetic variants of unknown significance, and vulnerability to discrimination. As a result, informed consent, which can be difficult to obtain in dementia patients is essential when conducting genetic or biomarker testing (Chiong et al, 2021).

When to Offer Genetic or Biomarker Testing

Genetic testing should be offered to symptomatic patients who have phenotypes consistent with autosomal dominant inheritance, such as early-onset Alzheimer's, frontotemporal dementia, Huntington's disease, and prion diseases, especially when there is a supporting family history. Similarly, biomarker testing may be clinically valuable for symptomatic patients with atypical dementia presentations or situations of diagnostic uncertainty, regardless of family history. In asymptomatic individuals who are at risk (such as adult relatives of patients with autosomal dominant dementias), predictive testing may be considered, but counseling is essential to explain the absence of disease-modifying treatments and the potential life consequences of both positive and negative test results. At present, genetic susceptibility and biomarker testing for asymptomatic individuals are recommended only in research contexts, largely due to the potential harms associated with these tests and the lack of interventions capable of altering the disease's natural progression (Chiong et al, 2021).

Decision Making and Capacity Assessment Ethics

Dementia is a progressive condition that eventually impairs a person's ability to make independent medical, legal, and financial decisions. In the early stages, when patients retain decision-making capacity, proactive planning helps them maintain control over future choices and reduces stress on caregivers. Patients with mild cognitive impairment or early-stage dementia should engage in discussions with family members and healthcare providers about their overall goals. They should also complete advance directives and other legal documents to guide future decision-making.

In the moderate stages of dementia, patients often lose formal decisional capacity but may still participate in discussions about their care. They can contribute by expressing preferences and values that should guide their surrogate decision-makers. These conversations help align future medical and legal choices with the patient's wishes, even when they can no longer make independent decisions (Chiong et al, 2021).

Assessing Decision-Making Capacity

Ethical challenges in dementia care frequently revolve around whether a patient retains the capacity to make decisions. Clinicians involved in dementia care should understand how to assess capacity. In some cases—such as patients with prior mental health conditions or disputes over financial matters—psychiatric or forensic evaluations may be necessary.

Capacity is not determined solely by a dementia diagnosis or cognitive test scores. Instead, it is assessed in relation to specific decisions. A patient may be capable of making certain choices while lacking the ability to make others. Clinicians evaluate capacity based on functional ability rather than a general diagnosis.

A widely accepted model identifies four core abilities necessary for decision-making capacity:

- **Understanding** – The ability to comprehend basic facts about one's condition, proposed interventions, alternatives, and associated risks and benefits. This can be evaluated by asking the patient to restate provided information in their own words.
- **Appreciation** – The recognition of how this information applies to one's own circumstances. Patients can demonstrate this by explaining how a proposed treatment would affect them.
- **Reasoning** – The ability to compare options and consider consequences logically. This is assessed by asking how different choices would impact daily life.
- **Choice** – The ability to communicate a stable decision, which should remain consistent unless new information arises (Chiong et al, 2021).

Advance Care Planning

Advance care planning should be prioritized while patients still have decision-making capacity. This process involves preparing legal documents that grant authority to designated surrogates for medical, legal, and financial decisions. Choosing a surrogate is a significant decision, as this person must be capable of prioritizing the patient's values over their own personal beliefs when making decisions.

While advance health care directives are valuable, they should not be treated as a final solution to care planning. Patients often struggle to anticipate the specific circumstances they will face, and surrogates may lack clarity on what the patient would want in medical crises. Advance care planning should be viewed as an ongoing process, involving discussions about values and preparing surrogates for their responsibilities.

Failure to plan can result in default aggressive medical interventions, which may not align with the patient's wishes. Additionally, without legal documentation, families may face lengthy court proceedings to obtain decision-making authority. Many patients benefit from consulting an attorney specializing in elder or disability law to address legal and financial considerations before they lose capacity (Chiong et al, 2021).

Decision-Making for Patients Without Capacity

When patients lack the capacity to make specific decisions, surrogate decision-makers should prioritize any previously expressed wishes, whether documented in an advance directive or conveyed orally. If no explicit preferences exist, surrogates should apply the principle of substituted judgment, making decisions based on the patient's known values and past beliefs. If neither approach is possible, decisions should be guided by the best interest standard, considering what would provide the most benefit while maintaining dignity.

Healthy individuals often underestimate the quality of life experienced by those with chronic conditions. Even when patients lack formal capacity, involving them in discussions about care values can be beneficial.

Surrogates should understand that their role is to reflect the patient's wishes rather than impose their own preferences. This approach can help reduce guilt and regret. As the disease progresses, clinicians and surrogates should make medical decisions within the broader framework of the patient's goals of care. If treatments such as resuscitation or hospitalization are inconsistent with these goals, it may be appropriate to implement do-not-resuscitate or do-not-hospitalize orders.

Many states have established Physician Orders for Life-Sustaining Treatment (POLST), which provide portable medical orders that apply across healthcare settings, including emergency situations. Unlike traditional resuscitation orders, POLST forms require careful consideration and should be reviewed regularly to ensure they align with the patient's current condition and preferences. These forms are most appropriate for patients in advanced stages of illness and should complement, rather than replace, advance directives (Chiong et al, 2021).

By incorporating structured decision-making processes and early planning, dementia care can better align with patient values, reduce caregiver burden, and prevent unnecessary legal and medical complications.

Symptom and Behavioral Management Ethics

Early Stages: Balancing Independence and Risk

Patients with mild cognitive impairment or early-stage dementia often struggle to assess their own abilities in daily tasks such as driving, cooking, managing finances, and participating in political decisions. These activities are significant to their sense of identity but can pose risks to their safety, their families, and the public. Restricting these activities can also have consequences, including financial exploitation if control over assets is transferred to unprepared or unethical individuals. Additionally, limiting engagement in meaningful activities can increase social isolation, leading to depression and worsening cognitive decline.

No approach can completely eliminate risk, but clinicians and caregivers can monitor patients' activities to reduce harm while preserving as much independence and dignity as possible. Driving presents a particular challenge, as dementia does not immediately preclude safe driving, but the progression of the condition means that patients will eventually lose this ability. Many will lack the awareness to recognize when they should stop. The American Academy of Neurology provides guidelines to assess driving safety, but even with clear medical recommendations, conversations about restricting driving can be difficult. The involvement of family members and friends may help facilitate these discussions (Chiong et al, 2021).

Moderate Stages: Agitation and Disruptive Behaviors

Agitated behaviors such as wandering, accusations, nighttime disturbances, and aggression affect nearly half of dementia patients. These behaviors contribute to caregiver stress, interfere with personal care, and pose safety risks, often leading to the decision to transition from home care to an institutional setting. Such decisions are complicated by cultural expectations, family disputes over assets, caregivers' employment and personal responsibilities, and emotional commitments such as promises made to loved ones about avoiding nursing home placement.

In both home and institutional settings, disruptive behaviors can endanger patients and others. Mechanical restraints, including bed rails, are now widely discouraged due to their association with increased agitation, physical injury, and the masking of treatable conditions such as delirium. If restraints are deemed necessary for safety, they should be the least restrictive option and used only with informed consent, typically from a patient's representative. The need for restraints should be regularly reassessed.

Pharmacologic interventions, such as benzodiazepines and neuroleptics, require careful consideration due to risks, including worsened delirium, movement disorders, and increased mortality. The Food and Drug Administration has issued a black box warning for atypical antipsychotics in dementia patients. These medications should only be used when nonpharmacologic strategies have been exhausted, and their risks should be weighed against other considerations such as patient safety, quality of life, and the ability to remain at home. If medication is necessary, it should be prescribed only after an informed discussion of risks and alternatives, and state laws may require additional legal authorization for their use (Chiong et al, 2021).

Advanced Stages

Nearly all surrogate decision-makers for patients with advanced dementia prioritize comfort over aggressive medical interventions, yet many patients still experience burdensome treatments and hospitalizations that do not align with these goals. One example is tube feeding, which has not been shown to improve survival, quality of life, nutrition, or wound healing, and removes the pleasure of eating. Hand feeding is generally preferred. Ethical conflicts arise when surrogate decision-makers request tube feeding despite its lack of medical benefit. While clinicians are not obligated to provide interventions without justification, feeding and nutrition hold deep symbolic meaning for many families. These situations require discussions that address both the medical realities and the family's concerns about care.

Pain management is another challenge in advanced dementia, as patients may struggle to communicate discomfort. Caregiver assessments using validated pain measures can be useful in identifying and addressing pain.

Many patients with advanced dementia die in hospitals or experience frequent transitions between care facilities, which can be distressing and medically unnecessary. Hospitalization is often a default response to perceived emergencies, but advance planning and do-not-hospitalize orders can help prevent unnecessary transfers. Most conditions, including pneumonia, are best managed in outpatient settings due to the risks associated with hospitalization, such as delirium and infection (Chiong et al, 2021).

Responding to Requests for Physician-Hastened Death

Physician-hastened death, legalized in some U.S. states, generally excludes dementia patients because it requires both a six-month prognosis and the ability to make an informed request. Advance directives cannot be used to request this option. However, neurologists often receive inquiries about physician-hastened death, which can signal broader concerns about suffering, loss of autonomy, and burdening loved ones. Physicians should respond with empathy, explore underlying fears, and address unmet palliative and psychosocial needs. Treatable causes of distress should be managed, and referrals to palliative care, mental health services, or hospice should be considered. Advance care planning documents should also be reviewed and updated to align with patient and family preferences (Chiong et al, 2021).

Cultural and Societal Ethics

Additionally, the relationship between dementia care and broader societal norms is an ethical concern. Stigma and societal perceptions of dementia can create barriers to care and support. Ethical issues include advocating for better awareness, supporting research, and promoting dementia-friendly communities. Reducing stigma and fostering a more supportive societal approach can improve both the patient and caregiver experience.

Financial Effects

The financial burden of dementia can contribute to the fear and stigma surrounding the condition. A significant portion of dementia-related expenses stems from in-home care, nursing home care, and the loss of income due to unpaid caregiving. These costs primarily address impairments in activities of daily living and are generally not covered by medical insurance, leaving families to bear the financial responsibility. Many American families are unprepared for these expenses, and misconceptions about Medicare's coverage for long-term care further complicate financial planning. Developing new models for financing and providing long-term care is necessary to meet the needs of both patients and their families (Chiong et al, 2021).

The Caregiver's Role

Family members and unpaid caregivers play a vital role in dementia care, often acting as essential clinical partners. Given the memory deficits associated with dementia, caregivers frequently provide critical details about the patient's history and facilitate the implementation of care plans. Caregiver strain and burnout can contribute to the decision to move a patient to institutional care and are also linked to an increased risk of patient abuse. While some studies suggest that caregiving negatively affects the caregiver's health, more recent research indicates that caregiving can also have positive emotional and physiological effects. The impact of caregiving depends on factors such as social support, cultural expectations, and the relationship between the caregiver and the patient. Women disproportionately bear the financial, emotional, and physical burdens of caregiving.

Many caregivers are unaware of available respite care, financial support, and other resources that can help them manage their responsibilities. Social workers can provide targeted referrals to these programs, helping caregivers maintain patients in home and community settings rather than transitioning them to institutional care.

As dementia progresses, patients often struggle to communicate their medical history, requiring caregivers to speak on their behalf during medical appointments. While the caregiver's input is essential, the patient's perspective should not be overlooked. Engaging with patients directly upholds ethical principles such as beneficence—prioritizing their well-being—and respect for their autonomy, even when their cognitive abilities are diminished. Clinicians should demonstrate through both words and actions that their primary responsibility is to the patient, ensuring that their voice is heard whenever possible (Chiong et al, 2021).

Abuse of Patients With Dementia

Dementia increases the risk of abuse, which can take various forms, including physical and psychological harm, sexual assault, financial exploitation, and neglect. Perpetrators may be family members, friends, or caregivers, and in nursing homes, resident-to-resident aggression is an emerging concern. Clinicians should be vigilant for signs of abuse, such as unexplained injuries, changes in behavior, social isolation, failure to meet the patient's basic needs, and financial exploitation. Assessing potential abuse may require interviewing the patient separately from suspected abusers.

A common misconception is that reports to Adult Protective Services require definitive evidence. However, in most U.S. states, physicians and other mandated reporters are legally required to report any reasonable suspicion of abuse. Once reported, Adult Protective Services typically conducts a home visit to investigate, though patients with the capacity to do so may refuse assistance. States also have designated mechanisms for reporting suspected abuse in nursing homes and other long-term care facilities (Chiong et al, 2021).

Socioeconomic, Racial, and Cultural Considerations

Older Black and Latinx adults face a higher risk of dementia than their White and Asian American counterparts, not due to genetic differences but because of social determinants of health such as limited access to primary care and early-life adversity. Delayed diagnosis in Black and Latinx patients is common, often resulting from barriers such as reduced access to specialists, cultural differences in perceptions of cognitive decline and caregiving, and clinician reliance on screening tools that do not account for cultural differences. Medical mistrust, rooted in both historical abuses—such as the Tuskegee Syphilis Study—and personal experiences of biased or inadequate care, further contributes to delayed diagnosis and treatment (Chiong et al, 2021).

Systemic Challenges in Dementia Care

Providing effective dementia care is complicated by the fragmentation of the healthcare system, where multiple specialists, hospitals, and nursing facilities often operate with incompatible electronic records. This lack of coordination increases the likelihood of preventable hospitalizations and contributes to the overall strain on patients and caregivers. Policy efforts have highlighted the need for more integrated care models that address the broad social, emotional, and medical challenges faced by patients and families.

One initiative in this direction is Medicare's introduction of Chronic Care Management billing codes, which aim to support care coordination beyond in-person visits. These codes cover activities such as medication reconciliation, communication between specialists, coordination with home- and community-based service providers, and comprehensive care planning. However, the extent to which medical practices can utilize these payments remains uncertain. Further research and policy development are necessary to create healthcare environments that respect patient autonomy, promote well-being, minimize harm, and ensure equitable access to high-quality dementia care (Chiong et al, 2021).

The Ethics of Artificial Intelligence

The increasing integration of AI in long-term care settings presents significant ethical challenges, particularly for older adults with cognitive impairment. While artificial companions are designed to provide comfort, companionship, and practical assistance, their use raises concerns related to deception, surveillance, informed consent, and social isolation. These concerns are further complicated by the rapid commercialization of AI technologies, which has outpaced the development of ethical guidelines and regulatory oversight.

Deception

Artificial companions simulate human-like interactions, often giving users the impression of genuine emotional connection. Many of these technologies are designed to mimic responsiveness, creating an illusion of companionship through movement, speech, and physical interaction. However, individuals with cognitive impairment may struggle to distinguish between authentic relationships and programmed responses. This raises ethical concerns about whether it is appropriate to encourage emotional attachment to an entity that lacks true understanding or empathy. Some argue that such deception, even if unintentional, could undermine personal dignity and lead to emotional dependence on an artificial entity rather than human relationships (Portacolone et al., 2020).

Surveillance and Privacy

Many artificial companions are equipped with sensors and tracking capabilities designed to monitor users' behaviors, detect changes in health status, and provide data to caregivers or medical professionals. While these features may offer safety benefits, they also introduce concerns about privacy and consent. Users may not fully understand or remember that they are being monitored, raising questions about whether their autonomy is being compromised. Additionally, there are risks associated with data security and potential misuse of personal information, particularly if such data is accessed by unauthorized parties or used for commercial purposes without the user's knowledge (Portacolone et al., 2020).

Informed Consent

Obtaining informed consent for the use of artificial companions presents unique challenges in dementia care. Cognitive impairment can affect an individual's ability to comprehend the nature and implications of AI-assisted care. Standardized guidelines for informed consent are lacking, particularly regarding when and how a proxy should provide consent on behalf of someone who may not fully understand their interactions with an artificial companion. Without clear protocols, there is a risk that users will be introduced to these technologies without adequately considering their preferences or best interests (Portacolone et al., 2020).

Social Isolation

While artificial companions are often introduced to reduce loneliness, their use may unintentionally contribute to social isolation.

If caregivers or family members come to rely on AI-based solutions rather than direct human interaction, older adults may have fewer opportunities for meaningful engagement with other people. Over time, this could lead to reduced cognitive stimulation and a decline in overall well-being. Ethical concerns arise when artificial companionship is used as a substitute rather than a supplement to human caregiving, particularly in settings where staffing shortages or financial constraints incentivize reliance on technology (Portacolone et al., 2020).

The Need for Ethical Guidelines

The rapid development and deployment of artificial companions have outpaced the establishment of ethical regulations, leaving significant gaps in oversight. Although organizations such as the IEEE and the World Economic Forum have advocated for ethical governance in AI, practical frameworks for regulating artificial companions remain underdeveloped. This lack of regulation creates uncertainty about how to balance the benefits of AI-driven care with the potential risks to users' autonomy, privacy, and emotional well-being.

Addressing these ethical concerns requires a multidisciplinary approach that includes policymakers, healthcare providers, AI developers, and caregivers. Guidelines should prioritize transparency in AI design, clear protocols for obtaining informed consent, and safeguards against excessive reliance on artificial companionship at the expense of human interaction. As AI continues to shape the future of dementia care, ethical considerations must be integrated into the design and implementation of these technologies to protect the rights and dignity of those they are meant to serve (Portacolone et al., 2020).

In this chapter, we explored the ethical challenges that shape dementia care, from diagnosis to end-of-life decisions. We examined the complexities of communicating a diagnosis, the risks and benefits of genetic and biomarker testing, and the ethical considerations in assessing decision-making capacity. We discussed symptom and behavioral management, highlighting the need to balance patient autonomy with safety. The societal impact of dementia care, including financial strain, caregiver responsibilities, and disparities in care, further complicates ethical decision-making. Additionally, we considered the ethical implications of artificial intelligence in dementia care, addressing concerns related to privacy, surveillance, and informed consent. Ethical dementia care requires a patient-centered approach that respects autonomy, dignity, and equitable access to resources. In the next chapter, we will build on this theory with some practical applications for empowering those affected by dementia.

Chapter 9

Empowering Those Affected by Dementia

In this chapter, we will define empowerment in the context of dementia and explore its implications for practice. This chapter will focus on four central themes: the state of being empowered, the process of empowerment, the role of the environment in fostering empowerment, and the effects empowerment has on various aspects of an individual's life. By understanding these elements, we aim to provide healthcare professionals and caregivers with the insights necessary to support individuals with dementia in maintaining control over their lives and preserving their inherent worth.

Empowering individuals living with dementia is a concept that continues to gain attention, particularly in healthcare and caregiving environments. Dementia, characterized by cognitive impairments that affect memory, thinking, and behavior, challenges individuals and their families. As the global population ages, the prevalence of dementia increases, prompting a need for approaches that respect the dignity, autonomy, and needs of those affected. Empowerment, in this context, refers to processes that allow people to have a greater say in their lives, make decisions about their care, and maintain a sense of identity and control, despite the cognitive and physical decline dementia may cause.

The concept of empowerment is not a new one and has long been associated with healthcare, particularly in chronic illness management. However, empowerment takes on a unique dimension when applied to individuals with dementia. As defined by the World Health Organization (1998), empowerment is the process through which people gain greater control over decisions and actions that affect their health. While empowerment generally refers to increasing personal control and choice, its application to dementia care requires careful consideration due to the unique challenges the disease presents, such as cognitive decline, behavioral changes, and the impact on identity. These complexities mean that empowerment for individuals with dementia is a dynamic and multifaceted process, involving not just the individual but their caregivers, healthcare professionals, and broader social support systems (Van Corvon et al., 2021).

Defining Empowerment in the Context of Dementia

To empower people with dementia, it is essential to define what empowerment means for this group. Empowerment can be understood both as a state and a process. In the context of dementia care, empowerment refers to the ability of individuals to maintain a sense of personal identity, control, and worth despite the cognitive and physical challenges they face.

The Alzheimer's Society has released "The Dementia Statements," a list created by people with dementia to reflect what they believe is essential for their quality of life. These include:

1. "We have the right to be recognized as who we are, to make choices about our lives including taking risks, and to contribute to society. Our diagnosis should not define us, nor should we be ashamed of it.
2. We have the right to continue with day to day and family life, without discrimination or unfair cost, to be accepted and included in our communities and not live in isolation or loneliness.
3. We have the right to an early and accurate diagnosis, and to receive evidence-based, appropriate, compassionate and properly funded care and treatment, from trained people who understand us and how dementia affects us. This must meet our needs, wherever we live.
4. We have the right to be respected, and recognized as partners in care, provided with education, support, services, and training which enables us to plan and make decisions about the future.
5. We have the right to know about and decide if we want to be involved in research that looks at cause, cure and care for dementia and be supported to take part" (Alzheimer's Society, n.d.).

A recent extensive review of the literature on empowerment for individuals living with dementia identified four critical themes: (1) the description of the state of being empowered, (2) the process of empowerment, (3) the contribution of the environment to the empowerment process, and (4) the effects of empowerment on other variables. These themes collectively highlight the complexity and dynamic nature of empowerment for people with dementia (Van Corvon et al., 2021).

The State of Being Empowered

The first theme explores the description of what it means to be empowered for people living with dementia. Empowerment in this context goes beyond simple autonomy or decision-making; it encompasses the person's ability to maintain a sense of self and personal identity despite cognitive and behavioral challenges. Being empowered involves feeling a sense of control over one's life, even when one's cognitive functions are compromised. This theme also reflects the recognition that people with dementia can continue to contribute to their communities, maintain meaningful relationships, and experience a sense of worth and dignity despite the effects of the disease.

Empowerment, in this sense, does not simply mean the ability to make decisions but also includes the acknowledgment of individuals' inherent worth. This theme is fundamental because it establishes that people with dementia, even as their cognitive abilities decline, retain the right to feel valued, needed, and respected in their personal and social lives (Van Corvon et al., 2021).

The Process of Empowerment

The second theme focuses on the process of empowerment, which is considered a dynamic, evolving phenomenon. Empowerment for individuals with dementia is not a fixed state but a continual journey, one that is influenced by both the person and their environment. In the context of dementia, the process of empowerment evolves as the disease progresses. During the early stages, individuals may still have a significant degree of cognitive ability and independence, allowing them to make decisions about their care, daily activities, and lifestyle. During these phases, it is essential to involve them in decision-making processes and encourage autonomy.

As the disease advances, however, the individual's ability to participate in decision-making diminishes. At this point, the empowerment process shifts to focus more on maintaining a sense of identity, worth, and dignity. Caregivers and healthcare professionals play a key role in this stage, helping the person with dementia engage in meaningful activities that reflect their preferences and values, even when verbal communication may be limited. The empowerment process, therefore, adapts to the changing needs of the individual while emphasizing the importance of respecting the individual's identity and preferences throughout the disease's progression (Van Corvon et al., 2021).

The Contribution of the Environment to Empowerment

The third theme emphasizes the role of the environment in the empowerment process. The environment includes the physical space in which the person lives and the social networks surrounding them. The environment significantly impacts an individual's ability to maintain empowerment, as it influences their opportunities for participation, autonomy, and interaction with others. A dementia-friendly environment, which includes features that promote independence, safety, and social engagement, is crucial in supporting individuals' empowerment. This includes physical environments that are easy to navigate, are free from barriers, and allow individuals to remain active and engaged in their daily lives.

Beyond the physical space, the social environment plays a pivotal role in empowerment. Family caregivers, healthcare professionals, and peers contribute to the individual's experience of empowerment by recognizing their abilities, facilitating their participation in decision-making, and providing opportunities for meaningful interactions. Furthermore, social support systems that are informed and sensitive to the needs of individuals with dementia can help preserve their sense of autonomy and identity, even as the disease progresses. The literature suggests that individuals with dementia often experience feelings of isolation and stigma, making a supportive and understanding social environment essential for maintaining empowerment (Van Corvon et al., 2021).

Effects of Empowerment on Other Variables

The fourth theme explores how empowerment can influence other aspects of a person's life, such as their emotional well-being, quality of life, and overall health. Empowerment has been shown to have positive effects on the mental and emotional states of individuals with dementia, promoting greater satisfaction with their care and improving their quality of life. When people with dementia feel empowered, they are more likely to experience a greater sense of self-worth, which in turn can reduce feelings of helplessness and frustration that are commonly associated with the disease.

Additionally, empowerment has been linked to improved interactions between individuals with dementia and their caregivers, as it cultivates mutual respect and collaboration. Empowered individuals are more likely to engage in conversations, participate in activities, and make their preferences known, which benefits both the person with dementia and their caregivers. The increased emotional well-being that comes from empowerment can also help reduce the behavioral and psychological symptoms often associated with dementia, such as anxiety, depression, and aggression (Van Corvon et al., 2021).

Implications for Practice

The findings of the literature review have important implications for practice in dementia care. First and foremost, they highlight the need for a person-centered approach that focuses on the individual's preferences, values, and experiences. Empowerment cannot be imposed externally but must be supported through collaboration, respect, and recognition of the person's inherent dignity and worth.

Furthermore, the review emphasizes that the social environment plays an important role in the empowerment process. Caregivers, healthcare professionals, and the community must be made aware of their role in building empowerment and be equipped with the knowledge and tools to do so. This may include training programs that teach caregivers how to support the autonomy and independence of individuals with dementia, as well as initiatives that promote a greater understanding of dementia within society at large.

As more people become familiar with dementia and its challenges, the misconceptions and fear surrounding the condition begin to dissipate. This shift in perception encourages a more compassionate and inclusive society, where individuals with dementia are seen and valued for who they are, not just defined by their condition. Communities that embrace these initiatives often report a ripple effect, with increased social cohesion and a stronger sense of community pride. Additionally, when people understand the signs of dementia, they are more likely to seek help sooner, allowing for timely intervention and better management of the condition. This awareness can make a significant difference in the lives of those affected, opening doors to resources and support that might otherwise remain hidden.

Empirical research is still needed to further clarify the role of the social environment in empowering people with dementia. Although the literature provides valuable insights, more research is necessary to determine how environmental factors can be optimized to support empowerment, particularly in different stages of dementia. Additionally, further studies should explore how specific interventions or programs can enhance empowerment for people living with dementia and improve their quality of life (Van Corvon et al., 2021).

In this chapter, we have explored the concept of empowerment for individuals living with dementia, highlighting its dynamic nature and its significance across the different stages of the disease. Empowerment goes beyond decision-making, emphasizing the importance of preserving identity, dignity, and autonomy, even as cognitive abilities decline. The interaction between the person with dementia and their environment, including the physical surroundings and social networks, plays a large role in facilitating empowerment.

Chapter 10

Emotional Support for Those Affected by Dementia

Dementia affects not only the individual diagnosed but also their entire family and caregivers. The emotional impact of the condition is far-reaching, as everyone involved must navigate an ever-changing reality. For the person diagnosed, the emotional toll can be overwhelming, often accompanied by feelings of grief, confusion, and frustration. Family members, including children, may struggle to understand and process their changing roles. Caregivers face their own set of challenges, often experiencing stress, exhaustion, and burnout. In this chapter, we will explore the emotional needs of those affected by dementia, offering guidance for family members, tips for supporting children through the transition, and strategies for caregivers to manage the emotional weight of their responsibilities, with the hope of offering some emotional relief for those affected by this disease.

Support for the Person with a Dementia Diagnosis

A person who has recently received a dementia diagnosis is likely to experience a range of emotions. These may include grief, loss, anger, shock, fear, disbelief, and sometimes even relief. For some, a diagnosis of dementia can bring a sense of clarity, as they now have an explanation for their symptoms. This realization can also provide them with the opportunity to plan for the future.

However, adjusting to this diagnosis can also bring challenges. The individual may feel anxious about the future, concerned about the episodes of confusion and forgetfulness that come with the condition, and distressed by the impact dementia has on their loved ones.

Dementia can lead to feelings of insecurity, as individuals may lose confidence in their abilities and judgment. They might feel as though they are no longer in control of their own lives and may struggle to trust their own decisions. People with dementia may also face stigma or feel that others treat them differently due to their diagnosis, which can negatively affect their self-esteem.

In some cases, the confirmation of dementia may lead to feelings of depression and anxiety. Various talking therapies and, when necessary, medication are available to help manage these emotional responses.

In addition to emotional challenges, dementia can impact other aspects of life, such as health, finances, employment, and relationships. These factors can contribute to a diminished sense of self-worth.

It's also important to recognize that those around the person diagnosed with dementia will experience their own emotional reactions. Family members and caregivers can support someone with a dementia diagnosis by recognizing and respecting their emotional state. It's important to listen carefully to what the person is feeling rather than telling them how they should feel.

Especially in the early stages of dementia, it can be helpful to encourage them to focus on what they can do and to incorporate lifestyle changes that may improve their well-being. This approach empowers them to maintain their sense of autonomy.

Support for the Family

Receiving a dementia diagnosis for a loved one is an emotionally challenging experience. It often involves significant emotional upheaval, complex logistical issues, and difficult conversations. A particularly tough obstacle can arise when some family members are in denial or refuse to accept the diagnosis. Their denial may stem from various factors, such as fear, a lack of understanding, or an inability to cope with the impending changes.

Denial can function as a powerful defense mechanism, shielding individuals from painful realities. Family members might resist accepting the diagnosis because it forces them to confront the vulnerability and mortality of their loved ones. It is important to approach this denial with empathy, understanding that it often arises from a place of love and fear (Better Health, 2024).

Misconceptions about dementia are common. Some may see it as a natural part of aging or fail to understand the full medical implications. Providing educational resources, such as pamphlets, websites, or consultations with healthcare professionals, can help correct these misunderstandings and offer a clearer perspective on the condition.

Sometimes, hearing the diagnosis and its long-term implications directly from a healthcare professional can make it more real for skeptical family members. It may be helpful to arrange a family meeting with the doctor or a specialist who can explain the diagnosis, prognosis, and care plan. The expertise and objectivity of professionals can offer valuable guidance and may be more readily accepted by family members.

If certain individuals' denial begins to obstruct the care process or foster a toxic environment, it may be necessary to establish firm boundaries. Clearly communicate unacceptable behaviors and their impact. Protecting the emotional and physical well-being of the person with dementia must always be the top priority. Setting boundaries is a responsible step toward ensuring the best possible care for the loved one.

Understanding Children's Reactions to Dementia

Children are often very perceptive and may notice when something is wrong, even without explicit explanations. Even young children can sense changes in family dynamics, such as increased stress, anxiety, or frustration. Unlike adults, children express their grief and distress in unique ways, and their emotional responses may fluctuate. A child might display sadness one moment and return to playing the next. While it may appear that they are unaffected, this could be misleading; children may still be processing their emotions, even if they seem to move on quickly (Better Health, 2024).

Children may ask difficult questions, such as "Will Grandpa forget who I am?" or "Will you get dementia, too?" It's important to be honest with them. Explain that dementia is a progressive illness, meaning that the person's condition will likely worsen over time.

Children's reactions to dementia will differ depending on their age. Below are common responses by age group and suggestions for providing support:

Babies and Toddlers (0-4 Years)

Common Reactions:

- Increased crying
- More clinginess
- Irritability or fussiness

How to Help:

- Maintain familiar routines to provide a sense of stability.
- Offer comfort by holding them or providing comforting items like a blanket or pacifier.
- Stay calm and speak in a soothing voice, as babies and toddlers are sensitive to emotional cues.

Preschool to 8-Year-Olds

Common Reactions:

- Clinginess and irritability
- Changes in eating, sleeping, or bathroom habits
- Difficulty verbalizing emotions like sadness or confusion

How to Help:

- Help them label their emotions, such as "sad" or "worried."

- Reassure them that they are safe and loved, keeping routines consistent.
- Encourage play as a way for them to express themselves, offering comfort when needed.
- Assure them that they are not responsible for the changes they are witnessing.

9 to 13-Year-Olds

Common Reactions:

- Increased anxiety, particularly about the safety of family members
- Strong emotions such as anger, guilt, or resentment
- Embarrassment or desire to hide the situation from friends
- A tendency to take on more adult-like responsibilities
- Withdrawal into solitary activities

How to Help:

- Encourage open, judgment-free conversations where they can express their feelings.
- Normalize their emotions, reinforcing that it's okay to feel upset or confused.
- Help them understand that illness is a natural part of life and not anyone's fault.
- Maintain their usual routine to provide stability.
- If appropriate, involve them in caregiving tasks but avoid overburdening them with too much responsibility.

Teenagers (13+ Years)

Common Reactions:

- Withdrawal and a desire for privacy
- Embarrassment or a desire to hide the situation from peers
- Difficulty expressing emotions or conflicting feelings
- Decreased academic performance or distractibility
- Acting indifferent or as if they don't care
- Fluctuating desires for more or less adult responsibility
- Feelings of guilt about future plans or reluctance to spend time at home

How to Help:

- Be open and honest, answering their questions to the best of your ability.
- Share your own feelings to show that vulnerability is okay.
- Continue with normal routines and activities to help maintain a sense of normalcy.
- Encourage conversations with trusted individuals, such as a teacher or counselor, about what's happening at home.
- Allow them to explore healthy coping strategies like reading, exercising, or talking to friends (Better Health, 2024).

Support for the Caregiver

Finally, those who are caregiving for someone with dementia will require additional support, especially due to the high prevalence of caregiver burnout.

Caregiver burnout is a condition characterized by physical, emotional, and mental exhaustion, often accompanied by a shift in attitude—from compassionate and caring to negative and indifferent (Cleveland Clinic, 2023). It typically arises when caregivers dedicate all their time and energy to caring for another person without ensuring that their own needs for support are met. It can also occur when caregivers push themselves beyond their capacity. Studies indicate that caregiver burnout is common, with over 60% of caregivers reporting symptoms (Cleveland Clinic, 2023).

Causes of Caregiver Burnout

This condition results from the cumulative pressures of caregiving and presents with symptoms distinct from general stress. Caregivers may experience profound exhaustion, irritability, or even emotional detachment from their responsibilities. Unlike stress, which is often situational and temporary, burnout permeates all aspects of life, leading to a loss of interest in previously enjoyed activities and a pervasive sense of emotional fatigue. This emotional depletion can manifest as hopelessness, accompanied by feelings of diminished accomplishment and self-worth, which starkly contrast with the initial commitment to caregiving. In some cases, caregivers may even experience resentment toward the person they care for, feeling unappreciated despite their efforts.

All caregivers face increased health risks due to the physical, emotional, and psychological demands of their roles. However, those who care for individuals with dementia experience even greater risks.

More than 11 million Americans provide unpaid care for family members or friends with dementia. In 2023, caregivers contributed an estimated 18.4 billion hours of unpaid care to individuals with dementia (Alzheimer's Association, 2024). Many caregivers choose this unpaid role out of a desire to keep their loved ones at home or a sense of obligation. While caregiving can be rewarding, it is also immensely stressful.

Caregivers of individuals with dementia face considerable emotional, physical, and financial challenges compared to caregivers of those without dementia. For instance, 59% of caregivers of individuals with Alzheimer's or other dementias report high or very high emotional stress (Alzheimer's Association, 2024). Spousal caregivers, in particular, experience greater burdens, especially as dementia leads to behavioral changes and a decline in functional abilities. The challenges are compounded when the person with dementia also has co-occurring conditions such as hypertension or arthritis.

Research shows that dementia caregivers are at a significantly higher risk for depression and anxiety than non-caregivers. The prevalence of depression among these caregivers ranges from 30% to 40%, with spousal caregivers showing a 30% increase in depressive symptoms compared to those caring for spouses without dementia (Alzheimer's Association, 2024). Furthermore, caregivers of individuals with dementia often report cognitive difficulties and are at higher risk of depression, particularly those caring for individuals with multiple behavioral symptoms.

The physical demands of caregiving can deteriorate a caregiver's health, increasing vulnerability to diseases and complications such as hypertension, weakened immune function, and poor sleep quality. Research indicates that dementia caregivers lose an average of 2.4 to 3.5 hours of sleep per week compared to non-caregivers (Alzheimer's Association, 2024). These caregivers are also at greater risk for physical health problems, including stress-related illnesses. They often struggle with physical care tasks and have a higher likelihood of requiring emergency medical attention and hospitalization. Studies also suggest that dementia caregivers may face premature mortality, particularly those experiencing high levels of strain in their caregiving roles.

Management and Treatment for Caregiver Burnout

There is no single solution for caregiver burnout. Recovery often requires multiple strategies to help caregivers feel rejuvenated and balanced again. Taking time for personal respite is not a luxury; it is a necessity for maintaining one's health and caregiving effectiveness.

- **Relaxation Techniques**: Deep breathing exercises can help reduce immediate stress by activating the body's natural relaxation response and lowering heart rate, blood pressure, and anxiety.
- **Meditation**: Practicing meditation for even a few minutes can clear the mind and induce calm. Guided sessions are particularly helpful for beginners.
- **Physical Activity**: Regular exercise, such as walking or yoga, releases endorphins that improve mood and relieve pain. It also helps improve sleep, which can be disrupted by caregiving stress.

- **Balanced Diet**: Caregivers should focus on a nutrient-rich diet, including fruits, vegetables, lean proteins, and whole grains, to maintain the energy needed for caregiving responsibilities.
- **Quality Sleep**: Establishing a consistent bedtime routine, avoiding caffeine, and optimizing the sleep environment can help ensure caregivers get restorative sleep and maintain emotional resilience (Cleveland Clinic, 2023).

Incorporating these stress management techniques into daily routines can significantly improve caregivers' well-being and, in turn, the quality of care they provide.

The emotional journey of dealing with dementia is complex for everyone involved. While the person diagnosed faces a range of emotional responses, family members and caregivers also experience significant emotional strain. Children, too, must be supported through their own confusion and grief. Caregivers, in particular, need to prioritize their own well-being to avoid burnout. Throughout this chapter, we've explored the importance of emotional support, practical tips for managing feelings, and the necessity of creating an environment of understanding.

In the Name of a Brighter Future

Dementia is a scary concept, but the more education we have as a society, the better chances we have of defeating it. Please take a moment to share this book with a wider audience so that we can get to that place.

Simply by sharing your honest opinion of this book and a little about how it's helped you, you'll spread awareness and help more people educate themselves about this devastating disease.

LEAVE A REVIEW!

Thank you so much for your support. I truly appreciate it.

Scan the QR code below.

Conclusion

As we conclude this exploration of the latest dementia research, let's take a moment to reflect on the key insights we've uncovered.

In Chapter 1, we discussed the different types of dementia and the risk factors associated with the disease, distinguishing between non-modifiable and modifiable factors. Chapter 2 focused on the difference between normal aging and dementia, providing insight into the signs of cognitive decline and how to assess them. Chapter 3 explored the tools and techniques for early detection, including biomarkers, brain imaging, blood tests, and the role of AI in diagnosing dementia.

Chapter 4 highlighted lifestyle interventions that can reduce the risk of dementia, such as physical activity, mental stimulation, and nutrition, with a focus on the Mediterranean and MIND diets. In Chapter 5, we examined the latest treatment advances, including FDA-approved medications and emerging therapies aimed at halting or slowing the progression of dementia. Chapter 6 covered holistic approaches to care, such as cognitive stimulation therapy, music and art therapy, and mindfulness practices, to support patients beyond medication.

Chapter 7 introduced technological innovations in dementia care, discussing how tools like remote monitoring and cognitive offloading can assist caregivers and patients. Chapter 8 addressed the ethical challenges in dementia care, including communication of diagnoses, genetic testing, decision-making, and the societal impacts of dementia. In Chapter 9, we explored the importance of empowerment, highlighting how a sense of control can improve the well-being of both patients and caregivers.

Finally, Chapter 10 focused on emotional support for those affected by dementia, offering strategies to help patients, families, and caregivers cope with the emotional and physical challenges of the disease.

It's my hope that you feel empowered with the knowledge you've gained. Armed with some of the latest research and insights, you can make informed decisions about dementia prevention and care. Whether you're caring for someone with dementia or seeking to protect your own cognitive health, understanding these nuances can aid in proactive management and decision-making.

My passion for helping individuals and families navigate the challenges of dementia runs deep. I am committed to providing you with reliable, easy-to-follow guidance and giving you the ability to stay informed about the latest breakthroughs. If you found this book and its insights helpful, please consider leaving a review. Your feedback helps others discover valuable information that could make a difference in their understanding of dementia and its treatment.

This journey doesn't end here—there's always more to learn and explore, and I'm here to support you every step of the way. I encourage you to read my first book, *Dementia Caregiving 101: Practical Strategies to Build a Support System, Navigate Medical and Legal Challenges With Ease, and Improve the Quality of Life For You and Your Loved One.*

Finally, I want to leave you with a note of encouragement. The strides being made in dementia research are nothing short of inspiring. There is a tangible sense of hope and positivity as we look to the future. Each new discovery, whether in the lab or through community initiatives, brings us closer to improving the quality of life for those affected by dementia. The knowledge and insights you've gained from this book are powerful tools. Use them to create a better future for yourself and your loved ones. Embrace each day with confidence, knowing that you're contributing to a world where dementia is better understood, managed, and ultimately, overcome.

References

Ackerman, C. (2018, July 25). *What is neuroplasticity? A psychologist explains*. Positive Psychology. https://positivepsychology.com/neuroplasticity/

Alzheimer's Association. (2022). *Special report: More than normal aging: Understanding mild cognitive impairment.* https://www.alz.org/getmedia/257803ff-0335-4882-a37b-c4acb77b1a66/alzheimers-facts-and-figures-special-report-2022.pdf

Alzheimer's Association. (2024a). *Special report: Alzheimer's disease facts and figures.* https://www.alz.org/getmedia/76e51bb6-c003-4d84-8019-e0779d8c4e8d/alzheimers-facts-and-figures.pdf

Alzheimer's Association. (2024b). *Donanemab for treatment of early Alzheimer's disease — News pending FDA review.* Alzheimer's Disease and Dementia. https://www.alz.org/alzheimers-dementia/treatments/donanemab

Alzheimer's Association. (n.d.). *Earlier diagnosis.* https://www.alz.org/alzheimers-dementia/research-and-progress/earlier-diagnosis

Alzheimer's Disease International. (n.d.) *Dementia statistics.* https://www.alzint.org/about/dementia-facts-figures/dementia-statistics/?utm_source=chatgpt.com

Alzheimer's Society. (n.d.) *The Dementia Statements and rights-based approaches.* https://www.alzheimers.org.uk/dementia-professionals/dementia-experience-toolkit/dementia-statements-and-rights-based-approaches

ARIIA. (2024). *Reminiscence therapy.* Australian Government Department of Health and Aged Care. https://www.ariia.org.au/knowledge-implementation-hub/dementia-care/dementia-care-evidence-themes/reminiscence-therapy.

Assil, Kerry. 2022. "Eyesight problems linked to dementia: what does that mean?" Assil Gaur Eye Institute Blog. July 26, 2022. https://assileye.com/blog/eyesight-problems-linked-to-dementia/.

Bryant, Erin. (2021, April 27). *Lack of sleep in middle age may increase dementia risk.* National Institute of Health. https://www.nih.gov/news-events/nih-research-matters/lack-sleep-middle-age-may-increase-dementia-risk.

Cao, G.-Y., Chen, Z.-S., Yao, S.-S., Wang, K., Huang, Z.-T., Su, H.-X., Luo, Y., De Fries, C. M., Hu, Y.-H., & Xu, B. (2022). The association between vision impairment and cognitive outcomes in older adults: a systematic review and meta-analysis. *Aging & Mental Health*, 1–7. https://doi.org/10.1080/13607863.2022.2077303

148   References

Chiong, W., Tsou, A., Simmons, Z., Bonnie, R. & Russell, J. (2021). Ethical considerations in dementia diagnosis and care. *Neurology, 97* (2), 80-89. doi: 10.1212/WNL.0000000000012079

Cleveland Clinic. (2023, August 16). *Caregiver burnout.* https://my.clevelandclinic.org/health/diseases/9225-caregiver-burnout.

Edwards, J. D., Xu, H., Clark, D. O., Guey, L. T., Ross, L. A., & Unverzagt, F. W. (2017). Speed of processing training results in lower risk of dementia. *Alzheimer's & Dementia: Translational Research & Clinical Interventions, 3*(4), 603–611. https://doi.org/10.1016/j.trci.2017.09.002

Espay, A. J., Espay, A. J., & Espay, A. J. (2024). Lecanemab and Donanemab as therapies for Alzheimer's Disease: An illustrated perspective on the data. *ENeuro, 11*(7), ENEURO.0319-23.2024. https://doi.org/10.1523/eneuro.0319-23.2024

Giulietti, M. V., Spatuzzi, R., Fabbietti, P., & Vespa, A. (2023). Effects of Mindfulness-Based Interventions (MBIs) in patients with early-stage Alzheimer's Disease: A pilot study. *Brain Sciences, 13*(3), 484. https://doi.org/10.3390/brainsci13030484

Graziosi, Dean. April 5, 2022. "50 Preparation Quotes to Get You Started On the Right Track." LinkedIn. Accessed March 12, 2025. https://www.linkedin.com/pulse/50-preparation-quotes-get-you-started-right-track-dean-graziosi.

Grueso, S., & Viejo-Sobera, R. (2021). Machine learning methods for predicting progression from mild cognitive impairment to Alzheimer's disease dementia: a systematic review. *Alzheimer's Research & Therapy, 13*(1). https://doi.org/10.1186/s13195-021-00900-w

Hao, J., Kwapong, W. R., Shen, T., Fu, H., Xu, Y., Lu, Q., Liu, S., Zhang, J., Liu, Y., Zhao, Y., Zheng, Y., Frangi, A. F., Zhang, S., Qi, H., & Zhao, Y. (2024). Early detection of dementia through retinal imaging and trustworthy AI. *NPJ Digital Medicine, 7*(1). https://doi.org/10.1038/s41746-024-01292-5

Harris, M. L., Titler, M. G., & Struble, L. M. (2019). Acupuncture and acupressure for dementia behavioral and psychological symptoms: A scoping review. *Western Journal of Nursing Research, 42*(10), 867–880. https://doi.org/10.1177/0193945919890552

Kiselica, A. M., Hermann, G. E., Scullin, M. K., & Benge, J. F. (2024). Technology that CARES: Enhancing dementia care through everyday technologies. *Alzheimer's & Dementia: The Journal of the Alzheimer's Association, 20*(12), 8969–8978. https://doi.org/10.1002/alz.14192

Kowalski, K., & Mulak, A. (2019). Brain-gut-microbiota axis in Alzheimer's Disease. *Journal of Neurogastroenterology and Motility, 25*(1), 48–60. https://doi.org/10.5056/jnm18087

Mackrani, Sanjeeta. (2023a, May 19). *Music therapy for dementia*. Alzheimer's Queensland. https://alzheimersonline.org/music-therapy-for-dementia-alzheimers-queensland/.

Mackrani, Sanjeeta. (2023b, August 28). *Cognitive Stimulation Therapy for dementia*. Alzheimer's Queensland. August 28, 2023. https://alzheimersonline.org/cognitive-stimulation-therapy-for-dementia/.

Mayo Clinic. (2021, June 30). *What new Alzheimer's treatments are on the horizon?* Mayo Clinic. https://www.mayoclinic.org/diseases-conditions/alzheimers-disease/in-depth/alzheimers-treatments/art-20047780

MoCA Cognition. (2023, July 25). *Mila and MoCA cognition partner up in battle against Alzheimer's and dementia.* https://mocacognition.com/moca-news/

National Institute on Aging. (2021, March 16). *Study reveals how APOE4 gene may increase risk for dementia.* https://www.nia.nih.gov/news/study-reveals-how-apoe4-gene-may-increase-risk-dementia

National Institute on Aging. (2023a, November 22). *Memory problems, forgetfulness, and aging.* https://www.nia.nih.gov/health/memory-loss-and-forgetfulness/memory-problems-forgetfulness-and-aging.

National Institute on Aging. (2023b, January 10). *Take care of your senses: The science behind sensory loss and dementia risk.* National Institute on Aging. https://www.nia.nih.gov/news/take-care-your-senses-science-behind-sensory-loss-and-dementia-risk.

National Institute on Aging. (2023c, November 20). *What do we know about diet And prevention of Alzheimer's disease?* https://www.nia.nih.gov/health/alzheimers-and-dementia/what-do-we-know-about-diet-and-prevention-alzheimers-disease

National Institute on Aging. (2023c, September 12). *How is Alzheimer's disease treated?* https://www.nia.nih.gov/health/alzheimers-treatment/how-alzheimers-disease-treated

National Institute on Aging. (n.d.) *Alzheimer's disease genetics fact sheet.* https://www.nia.nih.gov/health/alzheimers-causes-and-risk-factors/alzheimers-disease-genetics-fact-sheet

Ness Care Group. (2022, December 1). *What is neuroplasticity and how can it help dementia?* Atlas Care. https://nesscaregroup.co.uk/neuroplasticity-what-is-it-and-how-can-we-use-it-in-dementia-treatment/.

Phillips, C. (2017). Lifestyle modulators of neuroplasticity: How physical activity, mental engagement, and diet promote cognitive health during aging. *Neural Plasticity, 2017*(1), 1–22. https://doi.org/10.1155/2017/3589271

Portacolone, E., Halpern, J., Luxenberg, J., Harrison, K. L., & Covinsky, K. E. (2020). Ethical issues raised by the introduction of artificial companions to older adults with cognitive impairment: A call for interdisciplinary collaborations. *Journal of Alzheimer's Disease*, 1–11. https://doi.org/10.3233/jad-190952

Rohrer, L., Yunce, M., Montine, T. J., & Shan, H. (2022). Plasma exchange in Alzheimer's disease. *Transfusion Medicine Reviews*, 37(1), 10–15. https://doi.org/10.1016/j.tmrv.2022.09.005

Sense Medical Limited. (2024). *Paro - advanced therapeutic robot*. https://www.paroseal.co.uk/

Shang, X., Zhu, Z., Huang, Y., Zhang, X., Wang, W., Shi, D., Jiang, Y., Yang, X., & He, M. (2021). Associations of ophthalmic and systemic conditions with incident dementia in the UK Biobank. *British Journal of Ophthalmology*, bjophthalmol-2021-319508. https://doi.org/10.1136/bjophthalmol-2021-319508

Van Corven, C. T. M., Bielderman, A., Wijnen, M., Leontjevas, R., Lucassen, P. L. B. J., Graff, M. J. L., & Gerritsen, D. L. (2021). Empowerment for people living with dementia: An integrative literature review. *International Journal of Nursing Studies*, 124, 104098. https://doi.org/10.1016/j.ijnurstu.2021.104098

Verger, A., Yakushev, I., Albert, N. L., van Berckel, B., Brendel, M., Cecchin, D., Fernandez, P. A., Fraioli, F., Guedj, E., Morbelli, S., Tolboom, N., Traub-Weidinger, T., Van Weehaeghe, D., & Barthel, H. (2023). FDA approval of lecanemab: the real start of widespread amyloid PET use? - the EANM Neuroimaging Committee perspective. *European Journal of Nuclear Medicine and Molecular Imaging*, 50(6), 1553–1555. https://doi.org/10.1007/s00259-023-06177-5

Weiler, M., Stieger, K. C., Long, J. M., & Rapp, P. R. (2019). Transcranial Magnetic Stimulation in Alzheimer's disease: Are we ready? *Eneuro*, 7(1), ENEURO.0235-19.2019. https://doi.org/10.1523/eneuro.0235-19.2019

Young, Lisa. (2018, July 6). *18 Free cognitive assessment tools*. Eat Speak Think. https://eatspeakthink.com/online-assessment-cognition/#fast-gds

About the Author

Please allow me to introduce myself. My name is Debra Lewis. I am a 59-year-old wife, mother of four, and grandma of two. I have been a registered nurse for the last 35 years. I was also the primary caregiver for both of my parents before they both passed away three years ago from Dementia. Caring for my parents was a great honor and privilege. It was also one of the most challenging things I have ever done. That experience led me to get involved in online support groups for Dementia Caregivers. I did not know that I truly needed a place to grieve. God then led me to write about my experience and what I had learned during that time. I now attend conferences and meetings across Northern Arizona. I am speaking at the State Capital at a Caregivers Event. I continue to work as a nurse and will keep allowing God to lead me to help others going through what I did.

Printed in Dunstable, United Kingdom